VETERAN-CYCLE CLUB

CYCLING HISTORY NO. 2, VOL. 2

CHARLIE CHADWICK,
- FURTHER ADVENTURES
THE PRE-WAR CYCLING DIARIES OF CHARLIE CHADWICK

Edited by DAVID WARNER

The John Pinkerton Memorial Publishing Fund

Following the untimely death of John Pinkerton in 2002, a proposal was made to set up a fund in his memory.

The objective of the Fund is to continue the publishing activities initiated by John Pinkerton, that is to publish historical material on the development of the cycle of all types and related activities. This will include reprints of significant cycling journal articles, manufacturers' technical information including catalogues, parts lists, drawings and other technical information.

CYCLING HISTORY SERIES:-

The JPMPF Committee is aware that, apart from accounts of some popular machines, general information on most cycle marques is scarce. To overcome this scarcity we hope to encourage members, working with the help of other interested persons, to publish what information they have in a small book format. Hence the Marque Album series was launched with the publication of the Centaur book, followed by the Ivel book. We hope to follow these with many such publications.

At the same time, the Committee felt that there is a place for monographs on other aspects of cycle history in a similar A5 format.

Studies of early cycling organisations, such as the history of the Malvern Cycling Club, fall nicely into this category as does this work on Charlie Chadwick - Further Adventures, the second of the Charlie Chadwick volumes in the Cycling History series.

We are indebted to David Warner for transcribing Charlie Chadwick's notebooks and providing us with this unique insight on the founder of the Rough Stuff Fellowship, the Club for cyclists who enjoy byways and tracks.

Cyril Hancock, JPMPF Chairman

All publications are available through the V-CC Sales:. www.v-cc.org.uk
© John Pinkerton Memorial Publishing Fund 2014
Design and layout by Ray Miller
Printed by Quorum Print Ltd, Cheltenham, England
ISBN: 978-0-9575628-1-3

CONTENTS

FOREWORD

In my Foreword to Volume 1, I expressed the hope that there would be further volumes of the Charlie Chadwick diaries and drawings and I am pleased to say, because of the interest shown, this has now happened.

We all owe a huge debt of gratitude to David Warner for both preserving this valuable record of the inter-war cycle touring and also in painstakingly selecting material and arranging for publication. Charlie was very much a cycling mentor to David and other early members of the Rough Stuff Fellowship (founded in 1955). The exploits of Chadwick and others inspired a whole generation to seek out the remote paths and tracks at a time when this was deeply unfashionable in the cycling world.

I personally have done many of the routes described and many are still an adventure and physically challenging even with the benefits of modern technology. What comes across for me is just how much a tough day out was just viewed as the norm and not something special. I suspect if he learnt that 40-odd years after his death his diaries have been published he would simply be amazed.

I have been lucky enough to see the original diaries which are contained in a number of foolscap volumes. Obviously the quality of the drawings stand out, being amongst the best pen and ink drawings I have seen. It has been pointed out by Japanese art critics (where this genre is highly valued) that a good pen and ink drawing will convey the atmosphere, often by use of white space, that is what the artist does not paint. This is true of the best English drawings including Chadwick's. They possess that rare ability to make you see the scene when you visit or see a photograph through the portrayal by the artist. Just as impressive is the uniformly neat writing (achieved by using a template made of brass) which unfortunately cannot be successfully reproduced.

In the late 1990's the RSF published a small selection of drawings in their magazine. As the originals were done on lined paper, without the benefits of modern technology, they did not reproduce that well. So it is wonderful to see the high quality reproduction in these volumes.

So enjoy the second volume and if you can seek out some of these places on the bike many are still magical.

Steve Griffith
Chairman, RSF - The Club for cyclists who enjoy byways and tracks.

N.B. The RSF has very kindly made a donation towards the production of this second volume of Charlie Chadwick's diaries.

PREFACE

I think it is fairly safe to presume that many of my readers are not cyclists. I would go a step further and say that some are definitely anti-cyclist. But cyclist or otherwise, if there is anyone who cares nothing for the country, or are inclined with Charles Lamb to say *"I don't care if I never see a mountain"*, let him close this book now and pass it on. He is wasting his time.

But from you, my intending reader, I crave tolerance, and ask you to assist me by calling your imagination into play. I want you to get astride a lightweight bicycle and join me in long excursions beyond the precincts of brick and mortar to the purer atmosphere of the countryside. Happy days are ours! Some days we will enjoy the merry company of the 'We Are Seven'; some days we will be alone, just you and I, communing quietly, soberly, with the spirit of Nature. We will range the country round. We will be out today 'ere sunrise and spend a long day across the Marches, on the hilltops and in the valleys of Wales: tomorrow we will explore the forgotten tracks of the North Country fells: the day after we will contrive to lose ourselves in the leafy labyrinths of the Cheshire lanes.

Again we will shoulder our bicycles and take them through the exquisite limestone ravines of Derbyshire, or embark on a voyage of discovery into the shire of broad acres. What a choice we have! England – Ireland – Scotland – Wales! The mountain tops, the valleys, the rivers and streams, the plains and fields and woods, the moors, the coast, the sea and the lakes, everything in Nature lies open to us! Ours will indeed be a primrose path. We will refuse to consider the weather whatever it is – the best is glorious – the worst is not so bad, for do we not know how to make the best of everything?

Though I only ask you to lend your imagination, perhaps I ask too much. You will require a very vivid imagination to gloss over the deficiencies of my humble pen. These stories do not bear comparison to the stories lived; how futile they seem, how shorn of their deepest pleasures, how colourless! Again I crave tolerance for unloading this cargo of futilities upon your undeserving heads. I can only answer: "it is my best".

To you of the 'We Are Seven' who have lived many of these stories, I predict disappointment. How can I hope to recapture the spirit of those wonderful days and imprison it in the unromantic ink and paper of this book? The greatest, the most lasting pleasure of all is theirs only – memories. Can I reawaken those memories that are fading, can I set them dreaming of that autumn ramble in Chee Dale, of that sun-kissed day on the Peckforton Hills, of the alpine holiday in Lakeland, of that breezy dash into the Midlands, of springtime in Nant-y-Ffrith? Memories..... Images.... precious thoughts. They shall not die.... they cannot be destroyed.... They belong to you of the 'We Are Seven'

> *Long, long be my heart with such mem'ries filled!*
> *Like the vase in which roses have once been*
> *distilled;*
> *You may break, you may ruin the vase if you will,*
> *But the scent of roses will hang round it still.*

Moore

Charles Chadwick
496 Bridgeman Street,
Bolton,
Lancashire.
7 February, 1928

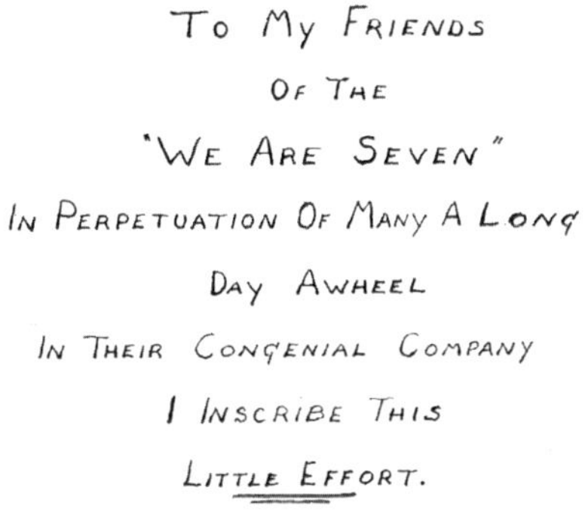

To My Friends
Of The
'We Are Seven"
In Perpetuation Of Many A Long
Day Awheel
In Their Congenial Company
I Inscribe This
Little Effort.

Fig. 1: Dedication to the 'We Are Seven'

INTRODUCTION

Welcome to the second volume of Charlie Chadwick's stories. This volume takes us much further into his adult life and indeed starts with what I believe is his absolutely best story 'Two – A Tandem and a Tyre'. This relates how in 1929 Charlie persuaded his friend Joe (who owned a tandem) to leave his girlfriend behind and become Charlie's 'stoker' for ten days in the southwest of England. It speaks volumes for Charlie's power of persuasion! Their subsequent adventures read like that old classic comedy book 'Three Men in a Boat'.

To comply with many requests for more drawings of Charlie's, the number of illustrations has been expanded and as a result they are not all related to the adjacent stories. Anyone who has enjoyed Charlie's earliest efforts cannot fail to be impressed with his collection in this volume – they are outstanding.

Sadly Charlie died in 1968 at the age of 64, leaving behind his secret treasure of stories and illustrations, painstakingly written in pen and ink, many of the drawings in the style of Patterson, who seems to have been his role model, to the extent that it is sometimes difficult to tell them apart. Everything that Charlie did was diligently recorded for our benefit. With his love of the high and lonely places, his knowledge of the countryside and all that grew in it, his expert photography, his knowledge of the byways and remote tracks it is little wonder that he was a founder member of the Rough Stuff Fellowship and indeed their first Chairman. RSF members still compete annually for the Charlie Chadwick Memorial Trophy photographic competition.

I mention his secret treasure of stories and illustrations for that was indeed what they were. Secret. Some years after Charlie died in 1968, his wife mentioned on one of our family visits to see her, that she had removed from her loft all Charlie's books, "and did I want to look through them before they were thrown on a bonfire?" I imagined she was referring to yet even more printed books, for he had a formidable library downstairs of travel and all manner of classic books, all well thumbed. I was quite stunned to be shown piles of ledgers and other original manuscripts, all dating from before his marriage in 1936.

Our thanks must go to the JPMPF production team, notably Ray Miller, Cally Calloman and Brian Hayward who have all played a key role in bringing this next book into our domain. Last but not by any means least I must record our gratitude for the financial contribution made by the Rough Stuff Fellowship towards the cost of producing this and the previous volume of Charlie Chadwick's work.

David Warner

PROLOGUE – ABOUT OURSELVES

I have never before tried to write consciously about myself or my wife except as a participant in some cycling or 'rough stuff' journey – in which I regard myself purely as the narrator, almost a 'third party' as it were.

Now that I am asked to describe a few plain facts I'm stumped !

Both my wife and I have long since lost the bloom of youth. I am almost 54 years, and she is over a year older. I was born within half a mile of this address in Bolton, and, except for a few years of wandering 'for

Fig. 2: Jo and Charlie

experience' as a young tradesman, I have never lived beyond this locality. My wife comes of farming stock, from the rich, reclaimed Martin Mere country between Preston, Southport and Chorley. My trade was the hard school of foundry work, with which I am still associated, though not so arduously, on the technical side, at Metro-Vickers, Trafford Park, Manchester.

The bicycle has been my only means of weekend and holiday travel since I was a child (being blessed with a cycling father), and unknown to me, my future wife was developing on similar lines. We met in that way, through the association of the CTC of which I have 36 years membership, and she about 30. Our married lives have passed 22 years.

The love of Rough Stuff, in our case, has never been for its own sake. Over 30 years ago I was tracing the rougher, quieter ways over the moorlands and mountains which, in the Pennine of Yorkshire, Lancashire and Derbyshire, in the Welsh mountains and Lakeland hills, are so fortunately placed for us, as to be within a few hours cycling away.

There are few essential things required for Rough Stuff Touring. As a youth I've crossed all the Berwyn paths in all parts of the year with nothing more than the bicycle (of course), an Ordnance Map and a good pair of brogues on my feet. An iron ration of food could be added. But Rough Stuff touring, to be enjoyed to the full, must be taken in complete independence of overnight accommodation. Experience long ago taught us to choose ultra-light, high quality camping equipment, eiderdown sleeping bags, paraffin pressure stoves, everything that will stand up to hard conditions of wind and weather, and yet provide reasonable comfort.

We have, in fact, geared our lives, as well as our bicycles, to Rough Stuff.

Our delight is not to cross untracked hill country with bicycles (we can do that better with walking boots and rucksacks – as we do), but to trace out the footpaths, the drove-roads, the ancient track-ways which are legion in our northern hills. These, at times, can provide a modicum of adventure!

I remember a day in 1943, when, free for a few days, I made my way down to Cynwyd Youth Hostel. The next morning I climbed up the south shoulder of Arenig Fawr between Llanwchllyn and Trawsfynydd. At the summit I congratulated myself on an easy climb, and a magnificent view, behind over the Valley of the Dee, and forward, to the long sweep of the barren Trawsfynydd valley, and the fine coastward ranges above Harlech Bay. I ate a picnic lunch beside a gaily fluttering red flag, and began a leisurely descent. I became puzzled to see many old motor vehicles at all angles on the hill slopes, then, here and there, dead sheep. Some newly dead. Suddenly, pandemonium was let loose. Shells whined on one side and the other, and exploded in great showers of stones and earth. To add realism I could hear the stutter of machine guns, though further away to the south. Of course I realised I had stumbled right into a target area of the Royal Artillery. Before I could look for shelter the salvo ended for the moment, and thoroughly scared I jumped on the bike and bounded down the rough moor with amazing speed. The guns did not re-open. In due course I reached a new concrete road and sped down until a barrier beside a watch tower stopped me. There I was met by a most ferocious sergeant who had the finest flow of language I had ever heard. Eventually I was told that had the look-out officer not spotted me on the hillside and stopped the War, I would certainly have been blown to smithereens.

When I reached the freedom of the public highway I realised that nobody had asked me for my identity card!!

If you know the Berwyns you will probably remember the green track from Pistyll Rhaiadr climbing across a cliff far above Llyn Llyncaws, with Moel Sych immediately above. One day in October, my wife and a friend and I packed our camping kits and began to cross the steep green ledge in a dreary drizzle. Suddenly my wife lost her foothold and, with bicycle too, began a dreadful slide towards the edge. I was too far below to help, but stood paralysed, waiting for the inevitable. Just as she reached the edge Fred, above, dropped his bicycle and made one wild grab at hers, to which she still clung. She went over the edge, but still clung on to the bicycle saddle, as to a lifeline. I raced up and between us we managed to get her back on the steep, treacherous path, none the worse, except for frayed nerves.

There was a Christmas a year or so before the war when we took camping kit up Nan Bield from Kentmere Valley in the hope of reaching Haweswater. A sudden mist completely blanketed us as we plodded up. Then we missed the track. All afternoon we floundered up the steep slopes, and every time we tried to descend we were met with a wall of crags.

We were forced higher and higher, onto a plateau, blanketed in mist, until even that began to turn yellow with the approach of night. There was a solid wall at the top. We chose the sheltered side, camped, got out the bucket, and I went in search of water, straight down the slope whilst my wife called to me from time to time to give me return direction. Scrambling amongst the broken cliffs I found a trickle, filled up, and returned without incident. And there, on the top of Harter Fell, we cooked our Christmas supper – even the Christmas Pudding, and camped cosy and snug until the morning. The mist was still heavy, but now we had a guide; we followed the wall which became a fence until finally the summit gate on Nan Beild was reached. Obtaining a campsite in Kentmere Valley, we went down to Kendal, and, the next night languished in a 'super cinema' for contrast!

Charlie Chadwick, written in 1958

Reverie.

IF THOU BUT TOUCH THE HILLS THEY SMOKE,
IF THOU BUT BREATHE UPON THE SONG,
THE SINGER'S WORD, THE HARPER'S CHORD
SHALL SOUND THE TRIUMPH OF THE LORD,
TO WHOM THE WORLDS OF ART BELONG.

Fig. 3: Reverie

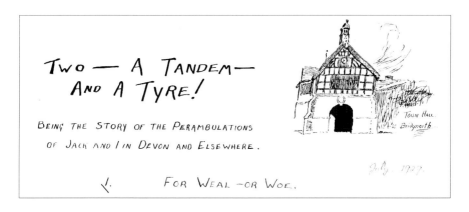

It is said that whatever one desires, if the desire is followed assiduously, and is not exaggerated, is within reach. Jack had formulated a great desire. The energy Jack put into his particular desire was out of all proportion considered in relation to his desire for work. I am the same. Whatever Jack and I possess in common is amply made up by the studious energy we collectively display in striving to avoid the enslaving demon, Work. There we shine as a twin planet of the first magnitude.

Jack and I had been bosom companions. That was before 'she' had come along and made him a half-unwilling captive. I say half-unwilling with due respect to all personal feelings, for, though we of the 'We.R.7'[1] – his companions – had striven might and main to keep him in our bachelor fold, not one of us could blame him when we first saw the cause of his downfall – smiling sweetly, and charmingly attired in rationals – behind his new tandem.

Until then, as I have said, Jack and I had been bosom companions. We had pottered together; we had toured together; we had even camped together, and together we had made tandem tyres sing on many a highway. So it happened when Jack's holidays came round I was hard at work – relatively hard, I mean. And when the time for my holidays approached, Jack was – relatively – hard at work. And Jack conceived a great desire – for another holiday. We were both keen; we would tour on tandem in Devon and Cornwall, camping, bathing, pottering. It would be a living fantasy of our old 'We.R.7' days – a drawn-out resuscitation of Utopia. We enthused jointly, and declared that life could not continue without a realisation of our dreams. As time drew nearer to my holidays, Jack's desire had kindled into a burning conviction that another holiday was his moral right; a sheer necessity. At work his desire began to show itself: Jack worked harder, displayed an unprecedented longing for it, craved to his employer for more. Such phenomena was bound to set the 'boss' wondering, so at the crucial moment Jack popped the momentous question. Of course he wasn't so blatant about it, for Jack is something of a diplomat when the occasion demands. He knew trade was very slack, and thereby lay his chance...... the matter was somehow squared, and for the intermediate days Jack's face took on a beam of pleasure.

There was a second hurdle to be jumped, but Jack's desire was equal to any obstacle. 'She' had to be appeased of course, and though I am not at liberty to divulge (even were I in the position to) how he gained her approval, I can say that a picture postcard a day, a pot of Devon Cream, and a lovely holiday gift figured largely in the ultimate agreement.

During the last few days at home we promised postcards and Devon cream lavishly. Relatives and friends demanded at least a card each; some could only be satisfied with a pot of cream, and by the time the last request had been registered, our obligations – for a mere ten days tour – had assumed mountainous proportions. It was jocularly suggested that we take an abode somewhere close at hand, acquire a gross of assorted views of Devon and a large consignment of cream, and with ample cider at hand to work up the correct atmosphere, spend our ten days posting cream and cards.

But joking apart, all the essentials of a wonderful holiday were there. A tandem, a complete lightweight camping outfit, and two real pals. On preliminary canters – I as 'Captain'. Jack as 'crew', we felt our old form creeping back, and never before had we romped along as we did on nightly excursions on that beautiful little speed-iron.

We left home on the Friday evening of a seemingly endless last day of work, with the prophecy to 'fetch' Devon by Sunday morning – for weal or woe.

> 2.   THE FIRST WOES.
>
> 'Leade on, good fellowe', quoth Robin Hood,
> 'Leade on, I do bid thee.'

Our old form came back to us immediately; with the harmony of dual effort we sped into the open country on glossy main roads of swinging contour. Often the legal speed-limit for mechanical vehicles was easily broken when a downward trend sent us free-wheeling beyond pedalling range (for we were geared low), and lane-ends, fork roads, and cyclists houses of call of many a year's familiarity dropped back into the limbo of forgotten yesterdays. Sunset hid behind the low green hills of Peckforton as we, with restrained wheels, traversed the hill-foot lane to the old, beloved campsite below 'the Gap'........ and in less than two and a half hours from leaving home we were cooking supper under the eave of our 'Itisa', forty miles distant. The spell was on.

I awoke to pleasant sounds and sight. The stoves were both roaring, breakfast was sizzling, and Jack was cutting bread. I lay stunned for a time at this new, unexplained magnanimity on the part of Jack. Perhaps he was turning over a new leaf. I hoped so, for here would be the Ideal Companion of my dreams, and a treasure if carefully and properly trained. I tried to train him a little there and then as I lay snug, but he retaliated with offensive remarks about laziness that was not at all consistent with the spirit of comradeship and helpfulness that I was striving to foster in him. In the end I had to leave the warm cosiness of the sleeping bag, and have a wash before I could breakfast in peace.

It was an ideal morning, the seeming herald of days to come, and in great spirits we packed up and continued the trek. The tangled network of lanes leading towards Whitchurch baffled us; we scorned to use a map in

Fig.4: .....We hummed along merrily ......

such a familiar district, and we soon got lost, wandering into the private grounds of Cholmondeley Castle on a beastly surfaced road that caused two spoke breakages. Close to the doors of the Castle, we were engaged in a quiet argument about the sheer lack of road knowledge the other possessed, when along came a gamekeeper, who joined the conversation. Our presence didn't rhapsodise him altogether, and he said so quite bluntly as he directed us to the nearest exit. Somewhat subdued by the unfriendly ways of man, we hied along the main road to Whitchurch, where Jack disappeared into a cycle shop for some spokes, and I made myself at home on the kerb.

An hour later, he awoke me. He had been having the spokes made, apparently. We skipped away at a rare pace across Prees Heath, and into lovely Shropshire country, over a red sandstone range of hills to Hodnet and Crudgington; seventeen miles in well under the hour. We had lunch at an old-world inn at the latter place, and chatted with a motoring party who were returning home from holidays in Devon. They had left sunshine and warm winds........ we carried on, dreaming about those warm winds and singing. That is, I sang. Jack croaked, although he swore to the opposite. Wellington's dirt and industrialism put an end to our duet, and from Wellington two or three dusty hills left us hot and sticky till Madeley and fair Salop – and what Jack calls his singing again. We glided down into the Severn Valley, where Bridgenorth quaintly climbs a steep hill with an ancient street and bridge. Rural England, trim and sweet with villages hardly touched by the despoiler, lay along that shining highway. We climbed to the hilltop border of Worcestershire and looked outward into crinkly country deep in trees; we descended in graceful sweeps to Kidderminster, which lies so near the heart of school-book history and looks so, but the Saturday afternoon crowds a-shopping in the narrow streets turned us away (speaking metaphorically), and we hied towards Worcester. Near the top of a hill, a mile outside Kidderminster, a whipping sound behind us caused us to dismount just in time to catch the rear tyre blowing off the rim. Although puzzled, we replaced it light-heartedly enough, and immediately forgot it. Little did we dream what that accident foreboded, how it was to change our holiday completely, and almost change our Utopia into a fiasco. Almost..........

The sun was shining and all along the road rural folks hawked strawberries. I acquainted Jack with my great yearning for a tea of strawberries and cream, but Jack disagreed. Such delicacies are alright for ladies and invalids, he said, but for elephants, wolves and cyclists on tour they are unhealthy. Whilst I was heatedly engaged in pointing out the peculiar vitamin richness of this succulent dish there was a sharp explosion abaft and we sank to the rim. Our hearts sank as well as we reviewed the catastrophe, and the strawberry and cream argument was forgotten. The rear tyre had blown off and the inner tube was in a sorry case. We stood looking at it until Jack, in a rare flash of real brilliance, suggested that we have tea (there being a place at hand), so we repaired thence. There was another cyclist in, an enthusiast on a 'sleeping bag' weekend (camping without a tent), and after due discussion, he decided to join us.

Jack was the mechanic, so he repaired the tube whilst I gave advice. He disregarded it, as he always does, and in a couple of miles the same thing occurred again. All along the way to the 'City of the Faithful' we had three more bursts, and the road was strewn with bits of inner tube and epithets. Our companion was the guide in Worcester, which was narrow, crowded and confusing. We had to view the great cathedral from without, then we sat on the river wall till the sun was low, watching the pleasure boats on the broad bosom of the Severn. We left the city by the Severn Bridge and joined a secondary road.

The road was all we could desire with common land of golden gorse, woodlands, distant views of the placid river, and far hill-woods – the Malverns. The evening had settled quietly as a summer evening does, our tyre troubled us no more, and we became at peace with the world and each other. The slow march of dusk turned our thoughts to camping, then we remembered – the groceries! Closing time an hour gone, Sunday tomorrow, and we hadn't an atom of food. The quiet evening became loud with the alternating voices of Jack and I, and the road fled under wheel in response to the urge on the pedals – the urge to reach a village shop. The alarm proved false. Upton-on-Severn was our saving grace and we laid in well and truly, continuing our ride in settled state once more. Came Tewkesbury, battlefield of long ago, with quaint old streets and a Saxon abbey that seemed still wrapped up in its turbulent history – and the Severn gliding placidly by. We lingered in Tewkesbury till twilight's deeper shades bade us move along, then made a gallant show on the Gloucester road. The gallant show came to a ludicrous end when the rear tyre flattened out. The Bogey had returned. The map came out, and a village by the Severn was settled on as our possible campsite; our friend bravely offered his bike so that I might go and make arrangements in advance. So I turned along two miles of lanes already summer-dark to the lovely little village of Deerhurst.

At a farm which hugged close to a beautiful old church I obtained smiling permission to camp in the 'second field by the river'. Blundering along a footpath, I found myself by the Severn, wide, deep, oily in the dusk, and somewhat hazy as to directions, I chose the nearest field, which was full of 'bumps', and soon had the little tent erected. The tandem pair came up with eggs and milk and the news that an old man had just dropped dead on the village green. Such cheerful news was followed by the inevitable arrival of a bevy of small boys who stood around with a look of awe on each face, and whispered to each other of our audacity in camping on 'Old Skinflints' field. Enquiries elicited the information that we were in the wrong field, and that 'Skinflint' was dead against camping on his ground; he was the small boys bogey, we learned.

Then along came the towing-path keeper, who verified the youngsters. remarks, and gave us an insight into the character of the fearful old monster whose land we dared to occupy. Apparently he was a power in the land, with fabulous wealth, a tremendous acreage, and a local magistrate to boot; consequently he held the means to crush any villager who dared lift a finger or say a word against him or his – and he never failed to use his power when necessary. All this might appear very terrifying, but it did not the least trouble the town-bred, proletarian minds of Jack and I. We said so, and implied that fifty village tyrants would not shift us that night, where-upon the towing-path keeper beamed on us. He said he had waited years for someone who was not afraid of 'Skinflint', and with embellishments suitable to the occasion, told us what he thought of the tyrant – what he had dared tell no-one before. So he departed, much relieved.

Jack gave me what he called a quiet lecture, stressing my shortcomings as a leader and when left to my own devices, recounting to our amused friend the numerous scrapes we had got into under my direction. Over supper a wordy battle ensued till at last words, 'Skinflint', and everything was forgotten in the soundness of slumber.

---

3.   A WET WAY : BRISTOL.

Once more I awoke to the pleasant sound of a 'Primus' stove, but the early riser was not Jack: Jack lay beside me slumbering lazily, though when our friend handed me Ovaltine and biscuits, he promptly awoke and demanded his share. Life seemed very fine just then! We went for a swim in the river which was quite warm, but not too clean and very deep, for at that point it is navigated by quite respectably-sized vessels, and when we returned our energetic friend had breakfast ready.

Just as we finished old 'Skinflint' came along. We saw his white smock in the distance and prepared a hearty reception, but beneath the smock and smock-hat walked an insignificant specimen (though of sour ill-tempered feature), that we were frankly surprised and disappointed. We had expected a ferocious monster with a whirl-wind of fiery oaths descending upon us, but instead we got what Jack contemptuously called "that" (with emphasis), and a surly request to "clear off". He went off to count his sheep, and finding all OK, he disappeared. So we packed up, went off to pay our dues at the farm, and to admire the beautiful church and a sweet modern miss who smiled (the girl, not the church) ……. Jack was relentless, and dragged me into a welter of lanes. We followed the map, and for once we reckoned right, by lanes of rare beauty, to the City of Gloucester, and to its old Cathedral, which we explored as best we could whilst a service was being conducted, for it was Sunday morning. The thing that struck me most at Gloucester Cathedral was the organ, which played with a richness and mellowness of tone that I have never yet heard the like.

Then it started to rain. Our chum departed for home, and we picked up a Bristol cyclist who took us to a little place along the broad Bristol road for lunch and shelter. Here he persuaded us to accompany him home, and so, for that day at least, we threw our hopes of 'fetching' the South coast to the winds. All along the thirty-five miles the rain poured down, and a strong headwind drove it under our capes till we were drenched. On the tandem we could have made light of the wind and short work of the miles, but our companion was slower, and ere Bristol was reached he was 'all out' in cycling terms. Suburbia led us to Clifton Downs, and we rode above the famous Gorge and suspension bridge, and descended on a winding road till the Clifton suspension bridge was far above in slender-threaded grace. Emerging onto wharves, whose main features were large bonded factories for tobacco – for all the world like cotton mills at home, we climbed heavily until the tumbled city streets lay below, and reached our host's house. There was nobody at home, and after changing our soaked footwear, and having a wash, we laid ourselves a sumptuous tea.

Our Bristol cyclist was no mean host, and it was late when he led us down his garden packed with full-bloomed roses to our tandem, introduced us to the vicar who carried on business in the church next door, and who was on fighting terms with him, and took us to a nearby shop which a delightful girl and her 'Mama' opened for our benefit. While 'Mama' served Jack, I got along fine with the daughter till Jack began a sermon about the time, and other material urgencies. The Bristol chap gave us explicit directions for the Wells road, but as soon as we bade adieu to him we went wrong and wandered through miles of uncharted suburban deserts. At dusk we found ourselves at Keynsham, five miles along the Bath road, and then a corrective byway ran us slap into the wind, and we got another drenching as we slogged along open-downs country. Darkness came on, and storm clouds gave their worst until a place called Marksbury was reached where we gave in – still forty miles from the Devon border – and sunshine and warm winds.......... We pitched our tent during a momentary lull, in a sheltered field, and discovered one or two uncomfortable things such as the loss of a stove valve which rendered the stove just useless cargo for the rest of the tour, and dampness on parts of the sleeping bags. We had another stove however, and nothing worried us for long on that eventful holiday. After the soothing influence of supper we turned in and slept as hardened campers should sleep.

4. SOMERSET AND DEVON AT LAST.

It was a tearful world to which we awakened next morning, and all around our tent were ridges, puddles and mud. "The third lumpy campsite in three!" Jack remarked. By the time breakfast had been disposed of, and all packed up, the rain had ceased and a high wind was blowing the clouds away.

We rolled over the Mendips, exposed limestone downland, in the face of the wind which blew away the lingering traces of dampness from our cloth-ing and set the busy housewives in prim villages a-hanging out their wash. At Chewton Mendip we settled down for half an hour with cigarettes and a map, but found that frittering time away on holidays is not half as satisfying and enjoyable as when at work. We joined a narrow lane that clambered up-hill for a long way until I was all 'hot and bothered'. Jack said that he was sweating too, but I reiterated that Jack never sweats behind me on the tan-dem, and there was a flare-up behind until we found ourselves freewheeling down a deepening dale for all the world like a main-road Derbyshire Dale. The little crags became taller, the road steeper, winding down, down...... our speed increased...... and almost headlong we plunged into Cheddar Gorge. There, mighty crags rose sheer from the tilted road towards scud-ding clouds, pinnacles contorted, and shining-grey cliffs, now smooth, now furrowed with age-old cracks and weathered gullies. Down below was quiet and still, and only the chasing clouds in the narrow strip of sky above gave movement to that picture of silent grandeur, Cheddar Gorge. Nowhere in Britain has limestone such a sight to show to the open sky, and nowhere in Britain's limestone nether-worlds are such places of lavish splendour as the Cheddar caves, the greatest of which we "saw and entered not" for two main reasons. Wookey Hole Cave in the village of Cheddar at the foot of the Gorge is commercialised, and visitors are tied to the expensive apron-strings of a guide. It is possible to hold an independent exploration, but the cost is prohibitive, and conditions require such things as writing in advance.

The second reason was more important. Cheese. That was the first thing that drew our attention on entering the village. It is advertised lavishly, but nobody ever needs to advertise it. It advertises itself. You can get it in paper wrappers, in boxes, in tins, in barrels, or you can seal it yourself in an iron-bound casket, but however you imprison the body, the soul of it will rise triumphantly. It is sold in little squares and triangles, and it is sold in full-grown cheeses; it is reared up and piled up in every shop window, and in some places it stands by itself unaided. Restraining a natural impulse to fly, we looked around, but Wookey Hole Cave, picture postcards, and bars of Cheddar rock (probably made in Manchester) seemed to be the only things on view – except, of course, the notorious cheese of Cheddar in various stages of decomposition. At the far end of the village, where the influence of the Cheese was not so keen, we bought bread and (Cheddar) butter, cakes, strawberries, and Cheddar cream, and ate the whole lot in the quiet seclusion of a little lane beyond sight and sound of Cheddar cheeses.

The sun came out. A little lane of exquisite beauty just below the Mendips took us to Wells, and to the crowning glory of that old Somerset city, the Cathedral. The magic of stone and stained glass in this work of many years commands the admiration of whomever views it, though again the blatant parade of banners of war and violent suppression aroused my rebellious blood. I enter the wonderful edifices of old England not with Christian spirit, and leave without the dawn of a prayer on my lips or in my heart. I enter for the sheer pleasure of magnificent architecture, and my reverence is for the preservation of stone, not the religion or the superstitious ignorance of priests. I hate them!

We reached King Arthur's Land. Glastonbury Tor, rising from the plains and crowned by a single tower, could hardly be likened to *"Many tower'd Camelot"*, but my willing imagination supplied the deficit, and I built it anew – as it used to be and is now in legend-lore. But romance became knocked off by the persistence of the hard headwind that spoiled our combined efforts. A rambling lane, perfectly level, led us through tiny marsh villages that have little changed from Alfred's days, and at the very village where the much-vaunted barbarian is said to have let the cakes burn we quenched our thirsts with cider shandies, a drink which Jack avows "spoils good cider". Sedgemoor, where, in 1684 the last battle was fought on Eng-

Fig. 5: Glastonbury Tor

lish soil, took us to Taunton, where we 'bought-in' for tea. In a lane off the highway we polished off a two-pound loaf, a bun loaf, a huge slab of cake, a tin of beans, tomatoes and a whole box of little St Ivel cheeses without turning a hair, and had we possessed more food that would have gone the same way. We were acquiring a holiday appetite. We promised ourselves supper in Devon, for already we had lost a whole day on our 'dash' south and had got into a carefree, come what will, attitude. A holiday attitude.

From Wellington we got a move on; the wind had dropped, and we did really well along miles of rolling highway, crossing the border of Devon, which, on that beautiful night, really did look like dreamy Devon at last. At Cullompton we found every shop closed except one, for it was early closing day. That one was a saddler's, and as dog biscuits and poultry food figured in the window, I suggested that a few dog biscuits for supper might improve Jack's voice on the principle that a moderate dog-bark is preferable to the hideous croak he calls singing. All the inhabitants turned out to hear the bother that followed, until, having used up all his expletives, Jack opined that we get along quick 'ere closing time in the next village.

We had just started 'getting along quick' when the rear tyre expired with a sigh, shattering our hopes of having cured the trouble. Patching it was a tedious job, for it was now all-over patches, and a new tube was imperative.

Jury Box.

—Taunton—

Fig. 6: Jury Box, Taunton

Once more we got swinging along at a rare pace, but the time grew later and not a village did we see. Closing time passed; we increased the speed; dusk fell, and 'blinding' with the fury that only a wild fear of going supper-less and without breakfast can produce, until, only ten miles from Exeter, we reached a shuttered-up village with a shuttered-up shop. At the side door our salvation was assured. For a further five miles we hunted for a campsite, asking a sweet little Devon lass who answered our knock at a wayside cottage door. She directed us to a farm along a private drive, and I found her an interesting and interested acquaintance until Jack soullessly dragged me away. The farm was really a small mansion, and everybody was in bed, so we decided to select a site for ourselves and do the asking on the morrow. Quickly enough were we acquiring that cool cheek that makes the successful hobo.

Without further ado we pitched and had supper – and just restrained ourselves from eating our whole supplies. As had become the rule, the site was stony, but even a few large clinkers in the small of the back obstructed our slumber little.

5.   THE   BOGEY   AGAIN.

We slept late. Each day the time had been creeping later, and during a soliloquy in the sleeping bag I wondered vaguely if we should pass the noontide abed before our holiday ended. Something would have to be done, and as Jack was showing his inherent laziness, I became perturbed at the possibility of actually being forced to get up first. This thought troubled me, for I hate getting up before Jack. The morning was calm until we began to argue about who should go and see the farmer, for if one of us did not go he would very soon see us. We wondered if he had already seen us, for the time was 9.30 am. The discovery that we had no eggs terminated the argument, and Jack went off for those requisites, and to pacify the farmer, while I prepared breakfast – and watched and listened for signs of conflict as a faithful pal should. He returned smiling, for our carefully prepared yarn had 'worked'; we were forgiven, and supplied with eggs, milk and water.

At 11 am. we moved away and soon reached Exeter. Whilst engaged in a merry game of 'touch and miss' with the traffic in the narrow tram-lined streets, our back tyre exploded with a roar, and with dangerous haste we pulled up. People appeared from nowhere in hundreds, and we found ourselves surveying the wreckage of a tube with a vast throng surrounding us. A nearby cycle shop sold us a new tube, and we walked to the Cathedral and forgot our bogey in the ecstasy of the magnificent pile – for a time. We had to take the wheel out to get the new tube on, so I held up the tandem while Jack fingered the chain and nicely blacked his hands. Then the chain somehow got fast between the gear wheels, resisting all his efforts to free it. Surveying his ruined hands, Jack begged me to have a try, though only after due deliberation did I consent, and with effort and oath in picturesque combination, we put it right between us and messed up my hands as well, to Jack's obvious relish. Then we sailed away, gingerly at first, but with increasing confidence until we were skipping away as carelessly as ever.

Four miles outside of Exeter, when we were speeding away down a steep, narrow lane, there was a great convulsive wriggle abaft; we skidded wildly across, and fetched up in the hedge. The back tyre had blown off again, and in the new tube was a great rent. Jack sang a swan-song in studious meditation, and I, sitting on the bank, decided not to disturb him. He was thinking! When Jack thinks, a tremendous amount of energy is required – more than he thinks is his share in pushing the tandem. At last he came out of his trance and said with great weight and finality "We shall have to mend it". I applauded this very obvious fact as the result of his mathematical brain, though the solution seemed as obscure as ever.

We mended it with meticulous care, and put the tyre on with equally commendable pains. We blew it up, and whilst pumping away ever so carefully, the tyre blew off on the unseen side and with a terrifying explosion, our brand-new, four-and-six penny tube passed out of existence. We gazed at it sadly for a moment, then we grinned. In two minutes we were roaring with laughter! Seemingly, there was no reason to laugh, but we saw the funny side. And that was the spirit all the holiday.

In the Cheddar Caves.

Exeter Cathedral.

In The

West Country.

The
Wellington
Monument.

Fig. 7: In the West Country

A companion who can laugh at mishaps; who can argue and stand argument in the best way; who can ride like a Trojan and face the 'music' with a grin; who can turn round when he is up against a continual and dogged 'run' of sheer misfortune and laugh outright; who can in that way turn a tour that bids to become a fiasco into the best holiday ever, is a companion to be treasured. A companion like Jack!

At this latest mishap we came to the conclusion that the tyre was an 'oversize', so Jack volunteered to go back to Exeter and get a new tyre and tube. We stopped a motorcyclist; Jack got on to the pillion, and I washed my hands, gave a youngster the remains of the tube, and went off to a cottage nearby for some light refreshment. An hour and a half later Jack re-

Fig. 8: Anstey's Cove and London Bridge, Torquay

turned with a new outfit, and then we soon got a move on, feeling strangely secure at last. Hunger came on; we bought in at a little village overlooking the Exe estuary, and in a side lane ate up everything we had bought and yearned for more.

We slid down to Starcross, a tiny resort on the mouth of the Exe, and in a post office, packed up the delinquent tyre and with it a biting criticism for Mr Dunlop. Thereafter, relieved to get it off our hands, we went on our way rejoicing that our troubles were at an end.

In the dull heat of afternoon we toiled up a steep lane till – presto! the sea, the warm South sea at last! A calm expanse of grey Atlantic, and across the river-bar, the bulwarks of Dorset; we dropped suddenly into little Dawlish, and pulled up at the end of the prom where the cliffs come down to the road. Passing motorists gave us an encore as we climbed up to the breezy top again, and in two miles sped down with screaming brakes into Teignmouth, where we landed onto the promenade. We were seeking a quiet bathing place for the sea was calm and enticing, but there was no quietude there, and once more we turned away, crossing the long excoriance [sic] that is called a bridge, and paying for it when we ought to have been paid if true values are the criteria. A monstrous hill reduced us to masses of perspiration, but the views held us in glad wonder, and we began to think the dream coming true in spite of being hopelessly behind our loose plans.

Once we found a sandy track, walked over a turfy common, and looked over cliffs at a tiny cove, beautiful, though marred by quarries and refreshment rooms. We flew down through suburbs and crossed a traffic-blocked tram termini to the little jetty of Old Torquay. A tiny harbour crowded with fishing craft in a picturesque corner of a wide bay where floated the low, grim hulks of several grey warships. Along the promenade we saw gardens and trees of strange, foreign appearance, for tropical plants grow freely at Torquay. This was an index to Devon weather, and in anticipation we rummaged out our bathing costumes and fingered lovingly the tiny phial of Lavender Essence that was to be our safeguard against mosquitoes. But no quiet bathing place could we find.

At Paignton, a tropical-looking attachment to Torquay, we held a hunger council, as it was long past tea-time, and of food we had none, but again it was Early Closing day, and we searched long and frantically for the necessities of life. Just beyond Paignton, a notice board outside a cottage announced that campsites were available, and upon enquiry, a buxom lady assured us that she could find us (for a consideration), the very place we wanted, and as her description tallied with our ideal, we hailed her as our deliverer, bought some more food, and hied away to our dream place.

As soon as we reached the place we knew that all was not quite as made out to be, but a small silky man with a silky voice virtually grabbed us, and while we gathered our wits, bustled us into a large, fenced off quagmire with tents and caravans all round the edge. We resigned ourselves to the worst, and bade our crafty-voiced guide lead us to our pitch, whereupon we were taken to a small space between two tents. That is the best I can call it, a 'space' marked off with sawdust and the number 6 painted on a piece of wood. It oozed with mud, but, as Jack philosophically remarked, it would at least be soft enough.

Our neat little Camping Club tent was the envy of the camp. The others were of the heavy canvas type, mostly tarred over, and pegged out by wooden pegs and innumerable guidelines. Soon we stood in the centre of an admiring crowd which eagerly swallowed every point of virtue about the 'Itisa'.

Then, like real he-men, we slugged off for a swim. As the lady had promised, we were on the field nearest the shore, but she had omitted to mention that there was a high embankment between which carried the busy Great Western Railway line, and entirely monopolised the view. When we

Fig. 9: Paignton Harbour

divested, the night became immediately chilly, and the sea was ever so cold. Five minutes was long enough to give us an attack of the shivers, and we returned, our child-like faith in the balmy seas of the West country shattered for ever.

Visitors still continued to inspect our camping complex while we, too hungry to take justifiable pride by showing them, prepared for ourselves a luxurious tea-supper, and got well down in our stock. The silky man came for his fee, which seemed preposterous. Jack, in his most disarming tones, hinted that he ought to be glad to pay us for the privilege we bestowed on him by using up a bit of his marshes, but he was a glib and hardened profit-eer, so the words went without effect. He suggested that we take a trip to the middle of the morass to read the camp rules, but without waders we re-fused to do so. Besides, camp rules are best read whilst leaving the site. We learned that we could hire a mattress, blankets, waterproofs, or have our breakfast at the house, but these things were of no use to us. We travelled complete.

We decided to go to bed early for once, and be up and away early on the morrow. We had to redeem ourselves somehow. Just as we were pleasantly 'passing over' a motorcyclist started his engine and drove the thoughts of blissful slumber from our minds for over an hour; his infernal persistence driving lurid language from our (usually) respectable tongues. The silence that followed was short-lived, for an express thundered past on its way to Plymouth, and shortly after another flew by with a piercing shriek – on its way _from_ Plymouth. In between golden little silences, one or two stopping trains rolled laconically by, but these we could have gladly suffered were it not that a party came in who had been on the spree in Torquay, and spoke not in whispers of it. This spirited – much spirited – crew yawled and shouted their way into the we sma' hours until we, tired of issuing threats and tirades, and weary of wooing hopeless sleep, arose, had another supper, and added our quota to the general pandemonium by starting our 'Primus' in full blast. This we kept going in savage glee till the whole camp turned on us, and we went to sleep happy in the knowledge that at least we had done our bit to the general welfare.

6. A Day of Diversities.

We lived up to our reputation, awakening later than ever (about 10 am.), and looked out to a gloomy world. A heavy drizzle had set in, and a mist, blowing from the sea, cast an air of depression over the camp. To some de-gree we welcomed this, for in its reflected outlook, silence reigned. From snatches of conversation we learned that many tents had failed to hold wa-ter, and leakages were many and uncomfortable. Our own little 'Itisa' was dry and comfortable, and breakfast was a slow orgy of drawn-out delight. We had an easy morning chatting with various pessimistically inclined and envious campers, writing belated postcards to neglected folks 'back home', and paying sundry barefoot excursions across the ooze to other tents, and once to watch the mists rolling in with the tide.

But at noon we tired of the camping ground and packed up, still in heavy rain. After duly digesting the camp rules, we got along with it down four miles of lanes; four miles of steep hills, deep hedges; four miles of honeysuckle to Brixham. South Devon is here at her best, even in the rain; old, packed town, tiny, snug little harbour full of craft, and the smack of the salt sea smarting in its sting with the rain on our faces. Brixham, in sheltered seclusion against the great Atlantic breakers; Brixham and the cliffs of South Devon; Brixham – Heaven, even in the rain.

We started for Kingswear, and climbed a barrier that took half an hour of hard tramping to overcome. On the top the rain redoubled its vigour, soaked us, blinded us, drove into our faces and our eyes, streamed off our bare heads. On a fearful gradient we tumbled down to Kingswear, stopping once to survey the panorama of the River Dart which lay below in a slanting veil of rain-mist like a sky beauty behind filmy curtains. At the ferry we waited for the clumsy traffic boat, and were sedately transferred to Dartmouth.

Like a breath of old Devon, quaint Dartmouth lives on the glory of the past. When England was in its struggling ascendant, Dartmouth was paramount; she sent ships and men – those bold Devon lads we read of in school books and in 'Westward Ho!' though in very truth cut-throats, pirates, and willing plunderers, as murderous as any demoralised Eastern usurper or Chicago gangster. Here were built the boats of the much-vaunted Pilgrim Fathers, and from the river they sailed to people the New World, as though the New World had not already suffered enough from the ravages of the white man. First the ravages of the white man's sword, then the ravages of his religion!

As is my wont, a bright idea germinated in my mind, and though Jack hardly applauded it, he agreed – to sail up-river to Totnes. That is the best way to see the River Dart. We went aboard, and after punting back and forth a few times between Dartmouth and Kingswear, we set sail up the river in company with about thirty dejected looking trippers – and a guide. The guide mounted a box, the audience gathered round dutifully, and in a sonorous voice he rolled out a lengthy history of every house, tree or rock along the route, enlivening the converse with a string of jokes as hoary as some of the rocks themselves. We gained an impression from him that the weather is always lovely, though, even as our guide quoted this a mist swept up behind, stinging rain came along, and a cold wind blew up in

Fig. 10: Brixham Harbour

chilly gusts. Everyone scattered for shelter, and we scattered as well, but really seizing the excuse to get away from what one of us irreverently termed 'the endless repetition of a gramophone record'. The majority of the passengers were of the dear old lady type, with a few subdued-looking men and one or two pairs of lovers, but never a girl who was interesting. But apart from that and the weather the sail was lovely. Even in the rain, the wooded hillsides smoking mist, the half-hidden creeks sheltering hamlets and often just a fisherman's cottage made lovely with whitewash, thatch, and roses, were of haunting beauty. As we approached Totnes the weather cleared, and a half-hearted sun gave a half promise. The boat, winding in and out first in narrow channels, then in wider bays, and giving us glimpses of higher, bolder hills, at length churned its way to a jetty, and we found ourselves at Totnes.

Totnes! I could write a eulogy on its steep main street, but I could not give my eulogy one rich Devon word to make it understood. Maybe it is enough to say we dallied there, and, remembering many sworn pledges, salved ourselves by posting one tin each of Devon Cream. Whatever my personal taste may be, who dares gainsay a waft of Devon sweetness on its way to a stifled Lancashire industrial town, to set dreaming – to brighten at least one soul shuttered therein?

The lanes from Totnes, and the many steep hills, gave us a ready excuse to linger, and to find a beauty spot to have a gorgeous tea thereat was our quickly satisfied guest. We were dispensing with a meal for the second day in succession, but, as I remember the vast quantity of necessities and delicacies we consumed each time, I doubt if our three meals a day idea was of any material gain. All that we saw of Ipplepen was a hillside cottage or two and an ivy-clad castle kept half-hidden in trees. We turned to Ashburton to buy in for the night prior to facing Dartmoor. The early closing demon was following us, for at Ashburton (quite a comfortable little town) we found every shop shuttered against us. We searched, we pried here and there, we banged at doors until in a side street bakery, a buxom dame beamed on us. Everyone came out and gathered round the tandem, and as we did our best to buy the whole shop's stock outright, opinions not always flattering floated in to us.

A rousing cheer, ironical maybe, but quite loud enough to make the much-flattered 'Amy' Johnson green with envy, followed us as we made our exit from Ashburton. We faced wild Dartmoor, walking up a fine hill with a fine descent, and an exquisite riverside ride to a really terrific hill that taxed us sorely. Came another descent, and with reckless speed we plunged down to a cottage, a bridge, a gate, a lovely little river-ravine, and another hill ahead that foreboded heavy work. Then came a dreadfully familiar hissing noise at the rear – and the back tyre subsided! For a time we didn't even look at it. We just sat on the parapet of the bridge wondering whether to throw ourselves into the river or not, and eventually broke into a weird dirge instead. Thus relieved, we set to repairing the thing.

A high wind brought scudding storm-clouds threatening overhead ere we fixed up again. Night was coming on, and our hopes of crossing Dartmoor that day were fading. We had got to the first 'elbow' on the next hill when we were hailed by a tandem couple in a little hollow, repairing exactly the same kind of tyre burst that we had so much experienced. They were bound for Ashburton, having crossed Dartmoor. We became even happy just then, for there was great comfort in the thought that we were not alone with our woes, but even as we stood there, singing blithely there was another drawn out hiss, and lo, our tyre flattened out of its own accord! The blithe song changed to a harsh croak, even worse than Jack's normal singing voice. Frankly, we were 'stumped'. Two new tyres and four tubes had been of no avail. At last it dawned on us that Mr Dunlop was not at fault. The back wheel-rim, though quite safe for the weight of a girl, was unsuited for two 'twelve-stoners' and a load of camping kit. Nevertheless we should have to put up with it. Their tyre repaired, the tandem couple gave us their sympathy which, though genuine enough, left us unmoved, and went their way while we occupied their little hollow and once more set ourselves to the task.

Rain came on, the tube was in a parlous state and the patches would not stick: twilight came over while we still struggled and got ourselves and the whole outfit wet. At last, realising that time and patience were required, we decided to find a campsite for the night. We walked back to the bridge and enquired at the cottage, but were met with an apologetic refusal and the ancient yarn of a disagreeable overlord was dusted and trotted out. Neither could we get eggs or milk. There was a beautiful common by the river, and there was a large notice which distinctly stated 'No Campers Allowed', but we were in no mood to be intimidated by notice-boards, and without a qualm we found a really delectable spot, a turfy clearing amongst great gorse bushes. With great trees in front and the river rushing noisily beyond a broken wall – with the wind swaying the branches, though we were sheltered and hidden from the road – with darkness growing – with the tandem broken down – abandoned by the wall – we were intensely happy, and ate such a supper that we left scarcely anything for breakfast!

After supper came a discussion. With lighted cigarettes and drowsy comfort inside the sleeping bags, we were able to make our plans. Clearly we would have to 'cut' North Devon out however much we disliked doing it. Our loosely planned tour had been cut to shreds, and now our only way was to move homewards. The morrow would be Thursday; our tyre had gone again, and as it was guaranteed, we decided to return to Exeter and try some other kind. Just as we were on the edge of sleep, Jack jumped up suddenly. He had heard something. We listened; the trees swayed and sighed and on the hills the wind made deep moans; spasmodic rain spattered on the leaves and on the tent; the river gurgled beyond the trees. After a moment we heard an irregular 'thud-thud', faint at first but coming nearer -------'thud...thud' on turfy grass, and rustling bushes, 'thud....thud....thud'..... and rustles, louder, nearer! We invited each other to look out and see, and we both displayed a marked preference for the warm eiderdowns. So, eventually, we both popped our heads over the door. The night was weird. Grey semi-darkness, with deeper shadows under the trees that waved branches like fantastic arms in the wind, and bushes that were but vague shadows themselves. 'Thud...thud' like a muffled drum close at hand, eerily mingled with wind-sighs and rain-splatters and river-gurgles. We peered into the grey, and...... there <u>was</u> something moving among the bushes! A faint, darker shadow amidst the shadows of the bushes, a shadow without shape. We stared hard, half in and half out of the sleeping bags, ready to jump – in which direction we hadn't considered. There were other moving shapes behind...... and the thudding was loud, rapid, now. The first form took shape, and with a snort, broke into the clearing where our tent was pitched. The snap of twig turned our eyes to the trees, and there we saw moving figures, four – five, maybe six. Involuntarily, I gave a shout, and immediately came a rush of forms by our tent – the thud of stampeded hoofs, and five or six wild ponies dissolved into the night.

It was an eerie, ghostly experience, and we laughed at it as we rolled back snugly again. The explanation was simple. The spot where we had chanced to camp was the evening rendezvous of a herd of wild ponies who roam the wastes of Dartmoor, and are very timid of man. They are rarely seen by the traveller unless he leaves the beaten track.

7.   FACING EAST.

'When sorrows come, they come not single spies,
But in Battalions!'   Shakespeare.

After a troubled night of spasmodic rain came troubled morning. We were up earlier – about 8.30 am., and were dismayed to find most of our food had gone in last night's supper orgy. A two pound loaf, half a pound of butter and a few biscuits were all we could muster, and after that we went hungry, promising ourselves the best dinner a man could hope for. With care and patience we repaired the tube, packed up, and were just about to move when the common-keeper came up. The turf was pressed down to the shape of the tent, but he had apparently no direct proof that we had camped on the hallowed spot, and after eyeing us very suspiciously, he went on his way. After walking up and down the fiercer hills, we rode tenderly into Ashburton and joined the Exeter road – the main road from Plymouth.

It was a beautiful main road with a swinging contour and a roaring wind behind; the temptations were many for Jack and I on that sporting tandem, and we quickly and conveniently forgot the rear tyre and bowled along for many a jovial mile, through rain and sunshine to Chudleigh where we raided a confectioners shop. With such delicacies to make the urge for lunch unbearable, we climbed gradually until we reached a little place with shelter and tea to drink, and views of the rolling lands o'er Dartmoor.

There came a breathless descent, on which we left amazed motorists behind in a frenzy of speed which the unrestrained impetus of the tandem lapped at nearer forty miles an hour – for a few brief minutes. A few miles from Exeter came the heart rending repetition of the past – another burst, and once more we added patches to carry us to the fringe of the city, where another burst compelled us to walk to the cycle shop. After explaining our case, the shop assistant tried every tyre of the same size in the shop, and every one we rejected as being too slack. The next size lower was too tight; we wanted to force it on, but the assistant would not let us take the risk of breaking the wire. The manager was sent for, and the whole stock was formally tried with the same result. With a new inner tube, we levered the lower sized tyre on whilst the manager wrung his hands, but we got it on in the end, and the shop-keeper, nobly standing by his guarantee, refused to charge for the new tyre. We thanked him and left Exeter in a happier frame of mind than we had known for days. We were assured of no more tyre bursts!

We still had a shred of the tour left, and agreed that we would make a homeward potter of the four days at our disposal, so we headed up the Exe valley, lapsing into song as our troubled past slipped away behind – forgotten things in a remembered land. Jack 'lapsed' into song – I 'ascended'. There lies the difference! We had covered five beautiful miles when a sharp hissing aft broke our song, and with suitable adjectives we dismounted. No need to look, we just knew that hissing could only mean one thing, the rear tyre. We wept in vexatious unison for fully five minutes, throated a funeral duet for a further period, then set to work. This time the tyre was too tight and had nipped the tube! We had a hellish struggle to get it off, and in replacing it we waxed hot and furious.

At Tiverton we bought new rim tapes, and just beyond the Thing went 'phut' again, and another half hour was wrestled away. Near Wiveliscombe, where the Exe and us parted company, a third puncture occurred, and while we were making faces to each other, an aged man and a young lady came along on 'dreadnoughts', and proffered help. We allowed the man to mend the tube and replace the tyre, which he did with infinite care, and guaranteed it. Then we joined a little lane route, hilly, but very, very pretty. We had no tea, but kept on, map in hand, through an intricate network of Somerset lanes till dusk found us at Cothelstone Hill, a 1 in 6 'teaser', we pulled up at a vicarage and 'put' the question to the old rector of the village. He had no land except a little paddock at the rear, and we could pitch there. We accepted, passed through a maze of privet trees and reached the paddock, a tiny, railed off, precipitous slope with more bumps to the square yard than any other we had met. It was a problem to pitch the tent, and one or two places were not as taut or as slack as they should be, but we had passed the stage of criticism long ago. Over supper, the rector came to chat with us, and proved a very well-informed chap on cycling and geographical matters, which is not what most parsons are, being too full of Scripture to allow of anything really sensible.

Tired enough, we rolled in and in spite of a host of bumps beneath, slept

8./ ACROSS THE SEVERN SEA.

like logs.

Yes, we slept like logs, if logs sleep late. And ate at breakfast like hogs until not a crumb was left. The rector had gone on his rounds, leaving a 'bon-voyage' with the housekeeper. Cothelstone Hill was a 'teaser', but on the top we got a magnificent view of the 'Severn sea', and all the wooded graciousness of the lovely Quantocks. Yet 'here only man is vile' – and I include woman, for a large crowd was gathered to hunt the stag. Men, women, and hounds, all out for the express purpose of hunting and rending one poor stag! Sport! Some of the elite of the land engaged in a vile pursuit of such a fine creature – Jack and I bubbled over in wrath, and expressed a pious hope that was intended for other ears, that they would break their precious necks at the first fence. Our wrath and the rear tyre subsided together, and another tyre-battle ensued ere we could slide down into Bridgewater.

We joined the dead flat road that runs to Weston-super-Mare, and made excellent time for the first dozen miles – till, in a village street, the tyre failed us once more. Our fingers nearly bled with the strain of pulling it off and replacing it. Buying a newspaper, we read that a boat was due out to Cardiff at 2.50 pm. – forty minutes hence, and we had 11 miles to go, which meant a speed of almost 20 mph to catch it. We jumped on and slogged the miles back in a great burst of speed like the old times, forgetting the tyre or hoping it would keep up. On the two mile length of promenade the people and the police stopped and stared as we flew past well above 'evens', dodging traffic and passing motorcars. We caught the boat with 3 minutes to spare!

The sail across to Cardiff was lovely, with sunshine and all the summer fashions parading aboard ship, insipid, bony, effeminate youths and maidens that showed a goodly proportion of 'figure', pretty and otherwise – disdaining the dusty figures of Jack and I. We played a merry game of avoiding tramlines, traffic and pedestrians through Cardiff, which, however, is an easy city to leave behind, and which boasts with justification of its new civic centre – including the just completed National Museum of Wales. The road northward through Taff's Well and Nantgarw, though industrialised, still contains figments of a once beautiful valley, and part of it was not new to me. We had missed dinner, which meant a gnawing hunger towards four o'clock, and a heavy investment at a grocery shop. We bought stuff for tea, supper and breakfast, but we ate the lot at a single sitting. Pontypridd was a black hell to us that hot afternoon, and nothing improved till we had seen the last of Merthyr Tydfil.

From Merthyr we climbed, and Welsh industrialism with its feverish squalor dropped like a cloak over the valleys behind. Up on the moors a few people lounged, drinking the wine of sunset air. Brecon Beacons were over to the east, just above us, and in sublimity they told nothing of the human miseries that peopled the valleys behind them and to the south, they were above the weary story of semi-starvation, of hovels huddled round silent pits that worked no more. Of unemployment and the blight of despair.

The ridge was topped at 1,400 ft., and we slid down Glyn Farrell into what seemed a land of enchanted things, if rivers and moors and moorland hollows, and valleys, are enchanted. To Brecon. The first instinct at Brecon was to go straight to a grocery store, and, unerring, we found one and repeated our laying-in habit. In twilight we climbed out of Brecon, shame-facedly, be it noted, we abandoned the Vale of Usk, and a short mile further on a farmer gladly allowed us to pitch our tent in what on investigation proved to be a hen-run. We found the exact spot where the hens had scratched the most earth away, and there we supped and slept and wondered what a smooth patch of land was like.

> 9.   THE GREAT DELUGE.
>
> 'Who had thought this clime had held
>   A deity so unparallel'd!'

Thus murmured Jack as he sleepily surveyed the outer world from the depths of his shorts-cum-jacket-pillow. I assented as I saw the steady drizzle descending from the triangular patch of grey sky above the tent door. So, with one accord, we turned over and slept another hour away. The grey sky and the drizzle still continued, and we made breakfast a long, lazy affair till nothing remained. Then a joiner 'rained off' from a nearby job came and we chatted away till noon brought a cessation of the rain. We packed up, and for eight beautiful miles rode dry-shod. At Llyswen we joined the Wye, and shaped our course up what I consider to be the most

beautiful section of a very beautiful river-route, the Wye Valley. At Llyswen too, we ran into rain of the real Welsh type, thoroughly wetting. The river was in flood, and it is worth a days heavy downfall to see the upper Wye in spate, bubbling 'over itself', driving between rock walls and over cataracts. At Builth we were soaked and hungry, and we found a place that did us well. Happily the tyre was on behaviour beyond reproach, so our spirits soared as the mercury fell and the rain settled to a solid downpour all the way to Rhayader. All the way to Rhayader – miles and miles of winding road by a river that kept our senses in delighted surprise at each bend.....
"oh, sylvan Wye thou wanderer through the woods" – sylvan yet in deluge!

A smoke and a 'breather' was indicated at Llangurig, six miles above Rhayader, for ahead were the mists and heavy gradients of Steddfa Gurig, 'Plinlimmon Pass'. A charabanc en route to Aberystwyth from Hereford unloaded a cargo of the most miserable-looking human beings imaginable. Their very features set Jack and I into hysterics.

Steddfa Gurig! Incredible, it seemed, that such a deluge could possibly

ABERYSTWYTH CASTLE.

Fig. 11: Aberystwyth Castle

continue for so long, but it did continue. It swept the moors in hissing douche, and the mists crept down as we crept up in the teeth of a wind that bit us. We helped a car out of a ditch and didn't get a word of thanks for it; we saw half a dozen others in a similar fix, and in anger we ignored appeals for help; we got drenched to the last stitch, and laughed thereafter that the worst could no more wet us; we fought our way all along the rippling summit of the Pass, and fought our way down when we should have coasted, till the lower slopes were gained and the wind lost its power. And at Ponterwyd we had tea after thirty-six soaking miles.

But worse had still to come – and better, withal! We started again loaded with the evenings foodstuffs, somewhat drier, but still with heavy rains. The land was very familiar now – we approached the lovely lands of many a holiday tour, a North Wales that is charged with memories and dear to me. Lovely, lovable North Wales roads! A downhill sweep took us to Llanbadarn where branched a lane that cut out Aberystwyth and took us well on the way to Machynlleth. From Bow Street to Tre-Taliesin something like a cloudburst descended on us, and in five minutes we reverted to that state which knows no wetter. The fury of it was appalling; roads were awash, streams rose to over-flowing, houses were invaded by irresistible torrents, and down the mountain-sides came newly born streams, over bushes and bracken and round the trees, down the walls, across the roads. We rode through it all like laughing, silly children, though we weren't silly because we might just as well carry on once we were wet, and we laughed because it was easier for us to laugh than to mope and grumble – and quite as effective. We had laughed at all of our ills in the same way.

Looking across the tide of the Dovey Estuary, we saw the clouds massed as black as night, and the wind from the sea driving them across Cader Idris – though Cader was invisible to us. As twilight approached the wind growled and grew, and whipped the trees into a sigh. A gale was coming in from the sea; we could see it in the quickening clouds and in the whining of branches; we felt the lash of the rain to our backs and on our heads, and twilight came early and went........ and left the night behind it.

A little farm at Glandyfi, four miles from Machynlleth gave us a campsite with sympathy ad lib. We only required the site. A friendly hedge staved off the force of the hurricane, and the farmers wife took in to dry as much of our clothing as we dared to let her take. We were left with little else beside a bathing costume! We camped in haste, and found ourselves upon tree-roots that stuck up beneath the groundsheet like logs of wood. But we dined well, and slept well upon them, in spite of the hurricane and the tattoo of rain on the tent.

10.   DELUGE — AND FAMILIAR WAYS.

Sorrowful tones and a scraping sound assailed my ears that Sunday morning at Glandyfi, and I looked round to see Jack industriously cursing himself and wiping butter from everything in his vicinity. It transpired that he had been sleeping on the butter all night, and half a pound of butter can be spread an amazing distance. Sleeping bag and groundsheet received the most plastering, and I thoroughly enjoyed listening and watching Jack work. It was a great pleasure to see him up at 8 am., a most unearthly hour to his way of thinking. And mine.

The rain was still inexhaustible, though nothing but a hard wind remained of the hurricane. Dry, warm clothing awaited us at the farm; we breakfasted, packed up, and were streaming along into Machynlleth by ten-o-clock. We tackled Corris Pass manfully, and marvelled at the volume of water in every stream. The rain was merciless and nothing we wore was proof against it; ere we reached the summit we were at last nights point of saturation again, and therefore happy. Happy with childish delight at every cold douche over our feet, at our streaming hair splayed like battered wheat over our heads. With a swoop we descended to Minffordd at the foot of the Tal-y-Llyn Pass, and with the wind now dead behind, we found it no more than a heavy drag. Cader Idris was a line of cliffs with a hundred streams down its hundred-crannied sides and the grey swirl of storm clouds enfolding the broken summit-crags. Tal-y-Llyn was far behind down the valley, a gloomy reflector of the gloomy heavens. And all the hills were lost in mists. The run down to Dolgellau was hectic. The brakes on the wet rims were a long ere they started to grip, and in that space we needed them. The many bends below Cross Foxes were taken at a steep angle that, each time, left us wondering why we did not conclude on our necks. In Dolgellau we shook ourselves much as a wet dog does after a swim, and went in a place for lunch.

After that came ten drenching miles of the Mawddach estuary to Barmouth. To anyone who will show me ten other miles containing so much beauty I will be forever grateful. Each mile impresses one as the culmination and the climax, the be-all and end-all of loveliness till the next takes you into further raptures, on and on, beauty transcending beauty till the mental outlook can take nothing more. Mountains and streams, a river intide, rocky banks and sandy dunes, ravines, woods, flowers and roses. These things in bewildering successiveness and other things unwritten give themselves to you on the Mawddach estuary.

From Barmouth we pursued the coast road and saw the darkness lifting from the sea. While we watched the mad torrent fling itself across the road when a bridge could take no more at Llanbedr, the sky turned from grey to broken white, and the rain ceased after a constant deluge of thirty-six hours. It seemed a great pleasure to ride unfettered, to towel our soaked hair and keep it dry, to feel our clothing like dish-rags no more!

Sunday, in Wales, a land as commercially dead as the proverbial dodo. Bigots have passed a law that no-one must open a shop on Sunday, and big-ots enforce strict adherence. A meal and a newspaper are the only articles allowed for sale, and in the case of the newspaper, to go by the average Sunday paper, that is the one and only thing which might be better prohib-ited. Wales, like the rest of Britain, must have its chapels and divorce court news, however! So at Harlech we were without cigarettes – a calamity! But we had been in Wales on many a Sunday......... a side-door of a side-street shop smuggled cigarettes to us with the air of criminals, and regaining the main street we stole past the sole policeman with skulking stride and burn-ing cheeks. We had evaded the law! And what a law!

The weather improved by leaps and bounds, which was unlike Jack's singing which always remains at a certain low level, and I had just reason to rebuke him. Thereafter, for several miles the puritan peace of Wales was disturbed. We had tea behind a hedge at Maentwrog, a sweet little place in one of the sweetest valleys in all Wales. We followed our usual custom of eating the whole of our stock, and thereafter found ourselves in the terrible position of being without food on Sunday in Wales. It was a hard climb to Blaenau Ffestiniog, but it was harder by far combing out Blaenau Ffest-iniog for food. We damned that law to the alleged inferno where bad Chris-tians are sent, and we knocked and punched a dozen side doors almost from their hinges ere one less biased lady, influenced no doubt by our haggard looks, provisioned us, bidding us hide all we had obtained ere we went out. To hide the stuff we got was nigh impossible, and a great bulge of brown paper covering bread was eyed by a policeman who stood at the very shop door. We grinned in triumph that he might deduce how happy we were, and rode away.

We tackled Garddinan Pass, a 1,400 ft. route of unpromising, industrial beginning, but blossoming into a glorious mountain crossing with a view down the Lledr valley that leaves one sobered and thoughtful. There rise the swelling sides of Moel Siabod in many colours, there on its little rocky eminence, hardly visible in the growing dusk, is 'Dolwyddelen's Tower', and there the mazes of the Dale delight the eye, charm the mind. *"What more seek ye, Wanderers?"*, quoted Jack as we tumbled down to the cork-

screw bends that took us to the river Lledr. The river Lledr in swollen pomp rushing down the rocks; the river shouting and chattering back at itself; the white fleck bearing down on the racing back of the flood; the thousand white streams pouring from the mountains in many a magnificent cataract of thirty-six hours growth; the washed shiminess of bare rock and fresh moss on cleaved rock; the roses clean and bravely blooming; the green finery of summer and all the majesty of summer in fields, in hedgerows; the scentedness of twilight – the dusky sky not yet swept clear of cloud.......
"What more seek ye, Wanderers?".

'Ye Olde Fish Inn' lent us the most beautiful campsite of our holiday; by the river the field stood and beyond sound or sight from the road. Boy Scouts, camping a couple of fields away, sent their chief to talk to us, and he was a man after our own spirit. Last night he had been washed out completely, and his patrol had been forced to fly to an old barn. The river had overflown its banks, and even while we talked the work of salvage was going on.

The ground was beyond reproach, and after previous sites, thought ourselves on a feather bed. We slept long.........

11.   THE LAST DAY.

Bank Holiday morning was so glorious that Jack got up first at the unearthly hour of 8 am., and not content with that, proceeded to awaken me. I protested vigorously, advancing the opinion that, as we had only ninety miles or so to cover, we ought to have a long sleep and a good rest. But Jack was keen on an early getaway and an easy potter, so Jack won. A swim was too risky in the raging river, but we dashed the sleep from us by means of an awfully chilly sit-down in a bubbling cataract, and then proceeded to polish off the usual gargantuan breakfast.

We packed up and slid down to Betws-y-Coed. Hot, glorious sunshine all the way up Dinas hill, with the Lledr valley beaming and the granite crescent of Moel Siabod above it, clear in the clear blue of the sky. At Pentrefoelas we turned north

Fig. 12: Lledr Valley

along the mountain road to Denbigh, and along that road, at a farm, was a notice board offering fresh cream for sale. We bought cream and half a quartern loaf. The lady was of the hardy mountain type, a type that a constant struggle with a barren earth has produced. She could speak no English at all, though she was apparently well under 40 years of age, and we could only surmise that she had recently come from the remote rockies of Shire-Carnarvon, or from the semi-waste hinterland of Anglesey. A man acted as interpreter, but she understood coinage so well that we found ourselves paying for bread at the rate of sixpence a pound. An argument ensued in Welsh from one side and English from the other, and the result was hardly enlightening to the detached observer who might be present. We eventually held our own and proceeded on our hilly way in happiness. From the first summit we beheld (as we had hoped) a magnificent prospect of all the principal North Wales peaks, laid out in line and behind each other like a mutilated saw-edge, and every one – even Snowdon, without a wisp of mist. At 1,584 ft. we reached the summit where, beneath a ridge, the little Sportsman's Arms Inn snuggles safe from the winds.

There was a great descent for about nine miles to Denbigh, and we held

Fig. 13: Snowdon and Capel Curig

not our impulsive steed, while real moving pictures unfurled before our eyes – the pleasant Vale of Clywd and its line of Moels, a brown chain of blunt peaks dominated by Moel Fammau.

We had lunch at Denbigh, and found the Pentrefoelas bread terrible stuff that we couldn't possibly masticate. We threw eighty per cent of it to a cow in a field, and waited a bit to see what effect it had, but the cow remained normal so we gave it the other twenty per cent. Denbigh was hardly three miles behind, and we were skipping away down the Vale of Clwyd with a fine wind aft, when there was a great sigh below. In automatic silence, born of practice, we proceeded to mend another puncture. After that we 'slipped it'. There was nothing to linger for on these roads, for these roads are as familiar as the back of my hand, and whatever charms may lie along them can comfortably be explored on a Sunday run. So we 'slipped it' through the long level valley to Mold, along the Wrexham road, then a lane and in turn the rolling road to Chester. On the outskirts of Chester we punctured again, and it proved the last of the series. We met a camping pair who often camp with us o' weekends. They were returning from a three day trip on the mountainous roads round Vyrnwy, and had a weary story to tell of Saturday nights deluge, of trying to light a 'Primus' with petrol, and of a consequent flare up inside the tent – with the tent closed up. To go by various adventures, these two certainly seem the most happy-go-lucky pair of a happy-go-lucky crowd.

After tea at a place midway between Chester and Warrington, we pottered home for 10 pm. – a reasonable time to end a holiday.

Two – a tandem – and a tyre! I ought to put "and three tyres", for three tyres and five tubes were the back wheels total in ten days. We must have had punctures, bursts or blowouts at least twenty times, and with as many heart-thumps, swan-songs, and ten times as many laughs!

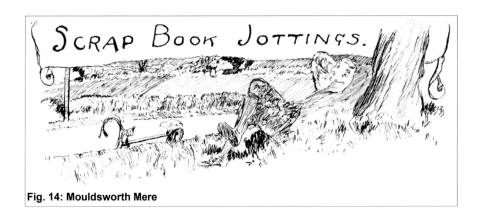

Fig. 14: Mouldsworth Mere

A Foreword

The following series of jottings are taken from a scrap book in which I scribbled limited pages at snatched intervals, diary-style. During the three mid-summer weeks ending the 14th July 1930, I found myself one of the vast army of the unemployed, and with the certainty of work to come after the above date, I devoted my time to a number of tourlets and two-day jaunts with camping kit, returning home on the days arranged to sign the register for my portion of insurance miscalled 'the dole'. If to no other purpose, these jottings go to prove the diversity of cycle touring and cycle-camping, the range of direction and district, and the adaption to the mood of the moment.

That these jottings are broken threads badly pieced, the reader will become aware, but, reader, consider how, when, and where they were written!

Mouldsworth Mere, Cheshire -Tuesday 26 June 1930

This is a great life; easy, luxurious, free, and with a fair measure of content. A strange twist of Fortune's fickly wheel has put me 'on the dole', and truth to tell, I don't care so much if I get a month or two of it! The 'dole' is no new experience to me, and in common with very many of the workless army, a feeling of indifference to work has crept upon me. After all, few sensible people prefer the commanding call of a day's labour to the sweet freedom of leisure. We are not afraid of work, but the clang of a bell or the harsh tones of a hooter is irksome. Like cattle we must go, and for wages that often leave us hardly above the level of cattle. Oh, I hate it!

The weather is very stormy, but the warmth of midsummer is in the storm and I am free for the moment, and now that the weekend crowds have gone and I am alone, beauty has settled over Mouldsworth Mere. I can bathe without fear of interruption, though a notice board fixed in an ideal diving place, warns bathers of impending contact with a police court. I have dived in from beside the notice, following the obviously marked footprints of many bathers, and found the water deep and cold enough to check any tendency to linger. Since bathing I have been to the farm two long fields away for milk and eggs, as lunch-time is near. After lunch I shall smoke and 'lie athynkynge' for an hour or so, then I shall pack up and find a quiet lane-route leading home. Tomorrow, after fulfilling Government require-ments, I shall turn away towards another campsite....... And thus I shall move till the hooter forces me back into the whirling vortex of workaday life. A month, perhaps two months.......... I do not care.

Of rendezvous I could write much. 'We.R.7' rendezvous I mean, and we two who remain intact and free[2] follow old procedure in such matters. By all manner of ways we go to meet each other, and all distances, which is quite natural because we live in different towns and sometimes work differ-ent hours. Thus it was arranged that I should meet Fred last Saturday at the Winster fork-road just by Haddon Hall at 6 pm. He would be out all day and could make a circuitous route, I could go straight from work at noon – work being on the right side of home for the district.

But at noon my unemployment and insurance cards were handed to me.......... for a week or two. An old gag, that 'for a week or two' tale, use-ful to the employer who isn't bold enough to tell you that he has no further use for you. I laughed, for I've heard that tale before – and I could afford to laugh – another firm had offered me a job..... in a few weeks.

I had some lunch at a place in Handforth that struck me as being of doubtful cleanliness, and then came in for a heavy rainstorm through Prest-bury and Macclesfield until, halfway over the Cat and Fiddle, the clouds broke up and omens of a beautiful aftermath began to appear. The climb to the summit at 1,690 ft. was dead easy with a good following wind, and the subsequent 'fall' for five miles into Buxton was a tale of brake-jamming and thrilling cornering at speed. Buxton and me don't agree with each other be-cause Buxton is very largely the home of that reactionary and immaculate set of people we call the 'upper-middle class', and I am a humble proletarian with proletarian ideas that are not humble, and a despiser of 'mode'. Wherever the fault lies, Buxton and I are not on lingering terms, and it was with a sense of relief that I slid down into the ravine of the Wye. I had time to kill, and there, by the shrunken river, under limestone crags, I found a pleasant way to pass a leisured hour. I joined a riverside path just where the main road climbs away from the Dales, and in sheltered woods scrubbed forty miles of travel from me, afterwards rejoining the main road by a

---

2   i.e. unmarried.

strenuous track. There were views from the top of Topley Pike of the great Dales-gashes and the green-brown waves of country above, dissected and intersected by grey walls of stone, picturesque if foolish. There was a sky of tender blue and fleecy clouds contrasting with the dark band on the eastern horizon, where the wind had swept the grey of early afternoon. From Taddington, down Taddington Dale to Monsal Dale, the loveliness of June filled the woods, aye, even the rocks, with midsummer beauty under a midsummer sun. I had tea at pretty little Ashford-in-the-Water, in the cottage of a pious old lady who relayed a jerky life-history that was conspicuous for its absence of thrill. She was an 'old maid', but quite a 'dear' providing excellent fare.

Just on time, I slid through Bakewell, by Haddon Hall, feted in romantic evening sunlight, and waited at the rendezvous for Fred, who was late owing to a troublesome tyre which still defied repair, so, deciding to seek an early site, we turned up Derwent Dale, into the Park of Chatsworth, where luxurious House and gardens lay dreaming like a mirage. At Edensor, the model village owned by the 'lord of the dale', the Duke of Devonshire, we cast about for a campsite, chasing a motor-car to some outbuildings, and, introducing ourselves to a prosperous looking man of the Bourgeoisie type, made our requirements known. We struck 'oil'; were shown into a paddock, modest in acreage, and rather strewn with brickbats, but in a beautiful position. We were on estate property. A couple of gamekeepers with guns in the crook of their arms strode up and set up a pleasant conversation of absorbing interest. Though not of the ruddy political complex that animates Fred and I, they had a freshness of outlook, a clearness of vision that we admired, particularly in men whose whole lives are bound up in servility to an overlord. They advised us to call at the Head Gamekeeper's place for milk and eggs – the owner of which had given us permission to camp. The house was a big one with a drive and gardens – and the car we had previously seen, at the door. His wife answered our rings, and proved a sweet little lady with a voice that fell like music on our ears. She gave us an over-measure of milk and double the eggs we had asked for, refusing definitely to take any payment at all.

In the very best of humour we turned in and in spite of many-cornered brickbats, slept like logs.

Fred is more energetic than I am. When I roused myself, and changed positions from a large stone in the small of the back to a larger one between the shoulder blades, he was busy replacing a wheel, having mended the obstinate tyre. The morning was gorgeous in warm floods of sunshine through June greenery of trees, and after the kind refreshing influence of a wash we

A DEW POND

Centuries Ago these ponds, circular in shape, were constructed in the limestone hills by puddling clay. Though only filled with moisture from the air they are never dry.

'A Wonderful ridge......'

Fig. 15: A Dew Pond and A Wonderful Ridge

settled down to our breakfast.

The gamekeeper's came up to resume the chat, and we marked a deer quietly grazing below the hilltop woods. I chanced to remark on the beauty of the creatures, and one of the men told me that she was doomed to die as soon as she came within gunshot. The reason is that the animals sometimes escape from their territory, and as they can never again be trusted to remain in bondage once they have broken loose, they are always shot by the first gamekeeper who sees them out of bounds. When I named my opinions on stag and deer hunting, controversy started to rage. Countrymen seem mostly reconciled to this infamous sport. We packed up and called at the big house again to pay our way, but the gentle-voiced lady would not hear of it, turning the talk to camping. She greatly admired the kind of life we lived o'weekends, and rapture illuminated her features as she spoke of her youthful days when she too lived the outdoor life and prosperity and luxury were beyond her dreams.

We chose a hilly route that capered across country, down Churchdale to Ashford-in-the-Water again, crossed the river by a pack-horse bridge, and on a bridle path of nasty surface up steep little Kirk Dale, and over rolling moors to Moneyash, where Fred punctured again. Moneyash is a pretty little village, situated just where a slight limestone depression marks the very beginning of winsome Lathkil Dale, and Moneyash has an old inn, where we sat over lunch listening to rustic tales and boasts from tongues loosened by copious draughts of muddy liquid retailed at fivepence per pint mug. For a myriad of men in many generations life has centred round the tap room table in a village inn, and when a hot sun beats down on arid limestone uplands there is as much to be said in favour of it as on those long cold winter nights when the cheerful fire and company of men counters the doleful, windy blackness of the hills.

There was a hot sun that afternoon, and white, heavy roads. We cut directly across the tiresome Buxton to Ashbourne highway, and ran down into a steep dale that held in its vice the white ribbon of a road that advanced to meet us. Earl Sterndale was the name of the village at its head, a quiet place just away from main roads; a place that possesses an inn with the quaint title 'The Quiet Woman', and displayed a picture of a headless woman on the sign. We agreed that a headless female is the only quiet one. Straight across the Leek-Bakewell road, in Glutton Dale, a white cart-way leaped to a hill summit, and that was the way we went, over the hilltops to catch the fragrance of cooler breezes, over 1,400 ft. up. Where a great view over the rippling country and Buxton opens out, Fred, whose tyre-luck was absolutely out that day, punctured again, giving me the opportunity to laze in sunny comfort for a spell. A wonderful ridge ride, a dip into a crinkled dale, a climb athwart a bank, and we crossed yet another tarred highway, the Leek-Buxton road ere we finally came to the Cat and Fiddle road again, and sped down to the outskirts of Macclesfield. Our mood was for byways, however, and the hopes of a swim led us three miles towards Leek to a canal that was all weeds. Then it was leafy lanes in lovely rural Cheshire to Gawsworth, and up 'Bluebell Valley' to Redesmere for tea. It was impossible to get a swim, not because of numerous forbidding signs, but be-

GAWSWORTH
RECTORY

(A ROUGH SKETCH)

Fig. 16: Gawsworth Rectory

cause Redesmere was too popular. Our appetite for lanes still unsatisfied, we went down to Wilmslow, crossed the common and passed through a gate to the pretty banks of the Bollin, to Greg's Mill, an old cotton mill all overgrown with ivy and toned to meet the finery of summer. Ten years ago, a friend who had a feminine attraction at Wilmslow, showed me Greg's Mill amongst other spots of rural charm in the locality, and though this friend is now 'safely' married and lost to the bicycle, those lanes and pretty places still give me occasional pleasure when I feel in pottering or reflective mood. The rest of the ride was through eighteen miles or so of suburbia, but it was a day to remember, and on some future winter night, to dream of. It was a mid-summer day.

Same Place, Same Day, 4 pm.

I have had dinner. I have laid me down awhile; I have swum in the warm mere, and now I will pack and potter home. I did not come by a direct way; I shall not go directly. I shall go by way of a Delamere Forest lane, and follow a cross-country course that will lead me over green pastures, by sparkling meres, through ancient hamlets and timbered cottages that sleep yet as a hundred years ago. There will be gardens and flowers on my way, and I shall travel slowly and alone. I have worked, and now's my time to play!

Groes Llwyd, Rhewl, Monday 30 June

At this moment of writing I am in no position to receive visitors, should visitors chance to call, a very unlikely event here. Laid down in front of my tent, my only article of clothing consists of a bathing costume tied round my middle, and that is 'on the limit' even in this modern age. There is a fine wind blowing down this Vale, and fluffy white clouds cross the hot sunshine, giving a fleeting chequer to the brown hills. The wind is warm and caresses me; I love those caresses on my body; they tone down the fierce rays; they make me feel luxuriously fit and well.

This morning I swam in the river, which flows smooth and deep not five yards from my tent. The river is cool, but not cold, and the wind makes little ripples which sparkle in the sun.

Through the trees, a hundred yards up the hillside, the white walls of the farmhouse are showing. Smoke is coming from a chimney; I hear ironed boots clattering across the cobbled farmyard; I see the small white, brown and black spots of poultry running about. There are cattle too, and the plaintive calls of invisible sheep higher on the hills.

Just behind me is a hedge shielding a meadow. Wild roses riot in the

Fig. 17: In a Delamere 'backwater'

hedge. The rest is green and brown, a hundred various greens on tree and pasture, a hundred browns on mountain slopes. On a moorland skyline above me four trees stand in wavering silhouette. Some people call this wilderness. *"O, Wilderness were paradise enow!"*

All weekend I have been following my inclinations, and following inclinations is a luxurious, often lazy game in midsummer. Inclination never leads me to work like many others; it entices me into sunny, riverside campsites, to spasmodic dips in the water, to semi-nude lazyings, and to frequent feeding! Just now it bids me write of what I see and sense.

On Saturday I explored the Peckforton Hills. I ought to say 're-explored', for those hills have given me many a days pleasure, rambling on woodland footpaths, bracken slopes, heather, red rocks and little forests of pine. I chatted with an informative farmer who gave me his history from the moment he learned to gurgle 'mama' on his mother's knee, down to June 28 1930 – that very day. Moreover, I learned the life-story of his father, whom (I gathered) was one of those great human benefactors that never emerge from their rustic obscurity. There are very many such people if we are to believe the evidence to be collected on every hand, and the great wonder to me is why the world has not improved much! The farmer directed me to the 'finest well in the world', and also gave me the whereabouts of the 'deepest caves in the world'. A man who could assert that two such magnificent assets lay within five minutes walk from his own doorstep was obviously a man worth listening to, and consequently I 'hung' on every word he said. He said a lot!

Fearful lest I should miss this marvellous well, I followed the farmers directions carefully. I found it beneath a bulging sandstone cliff, and it was running with a gurgling sweetness very musical to my thirsty senses. But the farmer, by oversight no doubt, had omitted to mention that this wonder-well was bricked in, and the door was securely locked. Somewhat sadder and thirstier, I set off to find the deepest caves in existence, for I still had a diminished quantity of faith. I found the caves. They were not very deep or extensive, but more in the nature of one extensive, low-roofed cavern with partitions and natural pillars supporting the rock roof. The floor was very uneven, and by the general appearance, I should judge them to have been cave-dwellings in the long ago. They resembled those in the grounds of Beeston Castle and the caves on Overton Hill, Frodsham. The farmer had remarked that it was impossible to explore them without a candle, but I scoured every corner with about six matches.

Same place, same day, after tea

I had made my mind up to move off deeper into the heart of Berwyn, but inclination deemed otherwise, and inclination was infallible to argument. I had another swim before tea, and found the water much to my liking. Even my swimming is lazy today, for I prefer to dive in near the upper rapids and float on my back without effort until the current takes me to the lower rapids. I shall go in again shortly. Winged pests are the only drawback in this Paradise of mine, and I've smoked about twenty-five cigarettes today in an attempt to keep them away. Cigarettes are a successful if expensive remedy with flies and midges, but I fear when the gnats get busy after sunset I shall have to seek another remedy.

To continue where I left off before tea

After satisfying my inclinations on the mid-Cheshire hills, I went down to Farndon for tea at a café just above the Dee Bridge. Whilst so engaged, in came a party of ten young ladies and four young gentlemen. I desire to put stress on the word 'gentlemen'. No doubt, I surmised, here was a Sunday school picnic adventuring abroad without their teacher, and the masculine section was gallantly leading the way with insipid jokes that received applause in such an admirably united and formal fashion that my suspicion was immediately raised. I went away convinced that the ten charming young ladies were pulling the immaculately-breeched legs of the four putty-brained young 'gentlemen', and enjoying it too.

As I had arranged to meet my own pal Fred, and the Wigan CTC campers at Nant-y-Ffrith, I shaped my course towards Gresford, a pretty little village just off the Chester to Wrexham highway, and on the way thereto trod, map in hand, an attractive lane route that became a cinder track, and later a footpath passing a very old, half-timbered hall. Gresford stands just above the Vale of Alyn, and the Vale of Alyn is much lovelier than people know. Only a tiny valley, but like a little gorge, profoundly wooded. But industrialism has played havoc with the stream, so that the naturally clear water is turned to an ugly brown liquid – the sweet gurgle of a lightsome river becomes a sluggish murmur of protest at man's bestiality to Nature.

And with a rankling in my heart to Nant-y-Ffrith, where crystal waters tinkling in summer playfulness bade me to forget my rebelling thoughts. A camp-fire, where a dozen lads sang songs to the darkening woods, where jokes and banter were as clean as the waters of the stream, and from which

King Charles' Tower; on the City Walls.   S' John's Ruins.

Fig. 18: Chester

we crept away one by one to seek awaiting sleep while the lonely fire glowed and died, and silence stole across the dell.

Like dreamy music the rippling sound of waters broke on our sleep, rambled through our awakening senses. The stream. To open our eyes and to see the rich gleam of sunshine along the meadow; to jump out, towel in hand, and let the silver water run through the fingers, and count our stone like misers with their gold. Ours the gold in sunshine, the silver in the fresh cold of clear water, the wealth in bounding health......and freedom. A feeling of sheer delight such as undreamt in stuffy towns: the heart expands till the heart could burst, and Life is grasped in greedy hands.....and lived. These I stake against a wealth of money. These things I have!

We cut stout sticks of ash and sought a way through the heart of Nant-y-Ffrith. A path by the stream faded out, and a tract of marsh, huge nettles that bit into our knees or scraped our arms, and philandering watercourse baulked by limestone rock spent the lovely morning away. We – exploring trespassers on forbidden property, searching every nook for beauty and finding it in great measure. Caves that burrowed dark and mysterious were searched with flickering matches, till we were caught in the very act of opening a door that seemed to lead to greater things. But keepers are only human, and this one yielded to the tinkle of coins; supplied us with candles; gave us the key, and left us to fathom the deepest recesses of the underground way. We emerged dirty and satisfied, prowled around the gardens and hothouses of the hall, and eventually hied back down the woods to our tents and lunch.

Again I was alone; again on the way; this time a quieter way up Nant-y-Ffrith and over the drive to the moorlands at Bwlch Gwyn. After tea at 'Ypento' in the company of two Liverpool chaps that I knew, I crossed the Horseshoe Pass, and in the clear air of evening detected the far horizon-line of Snowdonia. At Llangollen I stayed awhile at 'Bronant', the place where cyclists go as going home, where I am proud to know I am a favoured guest.....where Tom, my pal of a thousand memories has found his 'Joan'. Tom and 'She' and I walked down by the Dee to the Horseshoe Falls at Berwyn, and talked till twilight came. Then twilight lanes......and Groes Llwyd.

Tuesday Morning, 10.30 am. July 1 1930, Still at Groes Llwyd.

The first of July! Now summer marches forward in my regalia. Gone the tender evenings of lovable June; the reflected glory from May; the sweet end of Spring; blue eyed, lithe June......and July slides in with roses and heat-waves and the scents of new-mown hay already – suggested by the waving heads of meadow-grass. Summer is laid fully open!

The fine westerly breeze still blows, and the sky is broken into little clouds without a fear of rain. The shrunken river flows placidly, and the slight murmur of cascades come down on the wind. Not a soul can I see, but one or two quiet farms show in trees. There are the sounds of birds: I am alone, and I feel I'm in excellent company.

Last night whilst strolling leisurely by the river, I saw two girls of twenty-two years or so gathering wood, and perceiving that they were trying to catch my eye, I played up to them, and eventually helped them carry their loads. It was clear that they were strangers, and their dialect soon betrayed them as belonging to my home town, and on holiday. They were staying at a furnished bungalow in Rhewl with two elderly chaperones to whom I was introduced, and it was very obvious from the first that their weeks holiday was not as anticipated. They did not fit in with country like this, and frankly hated it. Their hate was vehement and brutally outspoken. The girls and I went up the hillsides till we stood amongst brown bracken and looked down on the glorious Vale and on sunset over the Berwyns, a marvellous scene to touch the human heart – but these girls were unmoved by those wonderful nature-pictures, preferring screen-pictures no doubt, in a stuffy theatre, or a crowded dance hall in Blackpool. Back at the bungalow, a gathering of the clans was held and village humour provided the entertainment till the clock struck midnight, and with the unnecessary sympathies of the feminine element, I went back by the moonlit lane to my riverside tent and the more contented company of my inclinations.

Same day, same place, 1.50 pm.

Having dinner. I shall have to return tonight, and I frankly do not want to move. Could have pierced the heart of Wales in these four days, but, though very fond of restless roaming, my frame of mind demanded the soothing quiet of some such spot as this, and these indulgent days have not been lost. There are tents half-a-mile down river, and the senior member of the party came to talk with me just before noon. He loved this spot, though his travel experiences were world-wide, and his occupation as boxing instructor at Liverpool stadium is not the type that usually begets lovers of solitude. A picture of man; an ex-champion with a Northern Counties Amateur Cup to his credit.

Went swimming again after, and the water was warmer than the air. There are hundreds of eels to be seen, water hens are quite tame, and now and then king trout jump after flies. The wind blows cooler. Now I shall go down to the village for food and cigarettes, and after tea I shall pack for home, tomorrow to seek fresh fields and pastures new.

Ingleton, West Yorks, Wed, July 2 1930, 10 pm.

At Ingleton! A strange campsite this, which I am sharing with six others in three tents, and about a dozen head of poultry. This is genuinely a hen-run, and a large, dirty bell-tent which (I understand) is occupied by week-end campers only, has become an admirable roosting place for the feathered tribe. When its human owners come to roost on Saturday I hope they enjoy themselves in it as much as the hens seem to do. I shouldn't! Our washing place is the River Doe which is reached by negotiating a minor precipice; overhead is the railway viaduct; on the hillside across the river, all Ingleton is free to come and view in detail the whole campsite, and altogether the place is emphatically not a second Groes Llwyd. The night is beautiful!

Yesterday I delayed my stay at Groes Llwyd until after tea. There is a magnetic charm abounding there, and sweet has been my stay – a lingering adieu is homage. To get home by midnight had been my first intention, but at Rhewl, barely a mile along, two 'hikers' from Liverpool hailed me. We exchanged greetings, jointly admired Winifred, a blue-eyed Norwegian from the village post office, and became entangled in a romantic chase around the farm buildings, much the kind of thing seen in a variety of settings on the screen. Winifred kept me occupied until 10 pm., when her father appeared rather suddenly, and with equal swiftness Winifred vanished. Apparently, dad was of the old school, a stern individual of the kind that makes you wonder how such a lovely girl can have such parents, and as I did not get along with him at all well, I returned to the two hikers who were wondering what all the fuss was about. Poor Winifred! I was lampless but an obliging youth with an ancient motorcycle offered to bring me a lamp from Llangollen. The lamp came, I settled down to supper, and the time sped until midnight – when I said goodbye and really went.

There is great charm in night riding when one is alone, traffic is gone, and the whole world around is still, quiet. One thinks a great deal on a great deal of things; there is little to fear on the roads, and only a superficial eye need be kept; cycling is unconscious, or, I ought to put, subconscious, and so the mind interprets the 'little noiseless sounds' and takes them out on the wings of fancy. The miles speed by; one becomes aware of that when one's eyes are startled by the lights of towns like Wrexham, cities like Chester, and by the grey spread of dawn. Then the sun comes up; the chill, grey hour disappears, and home is reached before the first factory blare awakens the sleeping towns of industrial Lancashire.

An hour or two in bed, a rush down into town ere 12 noon, dinner, and I

Fig. 19: Night riding

was away again, northeast this time – through Blackburn, Whalley, and along a quiet lane below Pendle where villages like Worston, Downham and Bolton-by-Bowland lie as pleasant surprises in folds of the low hills. The lane-way to Giggleswick, with its views of the Craven country, Pen-y-Ghent, Ingleborough, led me to meander. There is a well on the Kendal to Leeds highway at Giggleswick, which lies under a limestone hill and ebbs and flows at intervals of ten minutes or so (the guide books say), but neither ebb nor flow occurred in the ten minutes I stood there. Sometimes bare, sometimes of great attractiveness, always hilly, this high-way was my way, by Buckhaw Brow – 'a Shell famous hill' by the way – Giggleswick Scar, Clapham to Ingleton and tonight in a chicken-run. Tired, so I will off to bed now.

Bolton, Lancs, Friday 4 July 1 pm.
 I am home again. Having struggled into a collar and burdened myself with the horrid clothing men must wear to appease tailor-made

Fig. 20: Bolton-By-Bowland
Market Cross and Stocks

opinion in town, I have been to fulfil Government requirements, and now I must needs kick my heels until the Government pays me my insurance money tomorrow morning. To think that yesterday morning I strolled through Ingleton at a similar hour as, this morning, I was sneaking through the fetid by-streets of this sweltering old place! My people came to Ingleton by railway from a coastal resort, and, with others as well, we spent a drawn-out delight of a day in the glens which, in summer radiance of vernal things, compensated for the pitiful nature of the waterfalls. Pitiful they were compared with the wild fury of the streams as I have seen them after weeks of typical English winter, weeks of rain and storm I mean. Although my camping outfit provides very little limited luxury for one, five of us somehow managed tea from the stove, in the gill mug, and went away appeased at that! Four caught the 6.10 train bound for the coast, and I leisurely returned to my camp in a hen-pen. Leisured until the northern skies blackened with approaching storm. My outfit was snugly dry, and aware that I should have to pack up, I did it then with creditable speed, and took the lane route to Bentham. If I hoped to slip away from the track of the storm, I was soon disillusioned, for even as I admired an inky grandeur above Kingsdale, the heavens split with the crash of thunder, and deluge fell with all the fury of a July thunderstorm, piercing my flimsy summer clothing, drenching me before I got my cape unstrapped. But it is summer; it matters not, for the rain is warm and comfortable. What a lovely thing, this warm July deluge falling on a bared head! The sooty sky gradually cleared as I crossed Quernmore and dropped from the hills to have supper near Garstang, and after that came a smiling sunset and twilight into Preston. At Lostock Hall on the Leyland road, I know a house where the family breathes its life to the cycling spirit, and there I lingered with one I greatly regard but shall not name, [Jo[3]] until grey dawn dispersed the short summer night.

Expecting a great sunrise, I turned through the Rivington lanes to gain the hills that I might do justice to it, but sunrise proved a fade-out of the first magnitude, and a headwind was my tiny portion until, at 5.30 am. I came home.

Sunday 6 pm. July 6th Near Tebay

This is surely the greatest game! Here I am at tea beside a depleted mountain stream with the fells of Upper Lunesdale above and about me, crinkled monsters very like my old loves in the Mawddwy country.

Yesterday afternoon I met Fred and the Wigan boys at Walton-le-dale. Jo was with them on a short run, and we sat long at Mrs Whitehead's table

---

3   Charlie's eventual wife.

at Barton while he told us about his Irish tour just concluded. Then Fred and I went to swim in the canal which was agreeably warm. Following the Wigan lads, our route lay across Quernmore and along Lunesdale, all in the bewitching calm of evening. At one point we were fortunate to see black rabbits, white rabbits and the ordinary brown bunnies sporting together in a field. At Kirkby Lonsdale we joined the boys who were already encamped, and in the beauty of the night we made revel and talked, and in the early hours turned in, anticipating a swim on the morrow.

We awoke to a transformation next day, grey sky, a hopeless kind of drizzle and a cold wind. Surely we in the Northwest of England have a remarkable climate! The variety and severity of the changes in a single span of 24 hours make our opening conversations on the weather a really absorbing subject. In winter we are whirled through a succession of bitter cold comparable to arctic lands; winds that only arctic blizzards can boast the like, snow, sleet – a devilish compound, sleet, and rain; maybe a momentary burst of sunshine, maybe hailstones. We dance through a Spring of cold wind, hot sunshine and rain into a summer that inherits the name by courtesy more often than not. For weeks the sodden earth receives the English drizzle, a type of rain that once started, falls persistently, petrifies everybody with its gloomy atmosphere and makes the air 'muggy'. Then one morning we awake to a brilliant sunrise, and in a few hours we are in the closing stages of exhaustion from a sweltering sun burning with the fury of tropical intensity. For a day or two we roast o'days and boil o'nights till a breeze creeps up, gains power, becomes a gale, and our Indian heat-wave crumbles up in a violent thunderstorm. Drizzle returns and the whole process is repeated with variations to either extreme. Autumn is usually a period of drizzle without the warmth our summer gives, but with gales sandwiched between and the season ends with fogs, each one longer and of greater intensity than the last. Yes we are a long-suffering race and pretty hardy, for in such a cli-

Fig. 21: Devil's Bridge, Kirkby Lonsdale

mate the weak soon go to the wall to fulfil Nature's plan: the survival of the fittest.

How we grumble at it too – and how we revel in it! We have to be adaptable, and adaptable we are. At the first fall of snow out comes toboggans, bob sleighs, skis, and in the hills a few hours later organised snow sports are being keenly played by people who display the skill of experts with practice that cannot exceed a few odd days in the whole year. If one night the thermometer registers a few degrees below freezing point we may be sure that next day ice skates will appear in the shops, and from the same mysterious source as the ski's or sleighs will come forth a crowd of marvellous skaters who seem to have been born with a pair strapped on. The same night the annual curling and skating championship will take place by people miraculously gathered from all corners of these islands. Next day usually brings a thaw and all is as before, seemingly forgotten. The first warm day in Spring calls forth the very latest and flimsiest of dresses amongst womenfolk. Though next day the chances are on a return to winter furs or waterproofs. Waterproofs are the most important kinds of clothing in Northwest England. Again, the first sign of heat calls forth a multitude of bathers in a multitude of gaily coloured costumes, mostly experts as before, or we are regaled in our newspapers with pictures of river-parties, beach scenes, and picnics every bit as bright as those on the favoured Mediterranean coasts. Yes we are an adaptable people!

Rain is probably the most natural, certainly the most consistently abundant, element in our clime, so we hardly registered surprise, going down to the river for a swim before breakfast. A word of praise for the excellent natural swimming place we discovered. A hundred yards below Devil's Bridge and out of sight of curious eyes, we found a 'pocket' on the river varying from seven to twelve feet deep and overhung by limestone rocks that offered a variety of diving heights to suit timid and daring alike. The water is as clear as crystal with a bed of solid, smooth rock; the flow is placid, and it is quite possible to swim past the bridge or across the river. For non-swimmers the river shallows a short distance down, providing safe bathing four, three and, on the water flows, a diminishing number of feet. This is about the best river-stretch for bathing I know notwithstanding our favourite 'bit' on the Dee at Groes Llwyd, which is very dangerous to weak or non-swimmers. The one disadvantage of bathing during heavy rain was illustrated when we came to dry ourselves, the rain doing its worst as we did our best. Then breakfast in leisured comfort and a long siesta, drowsily tale-telling, and paying sundry trips to review photographs or hear of the latest touring adventures.

Fig. 22: Shap Fells

Towards noon the mists lifted from the hills and later the drizzle ceased. As we munched a lazy dinner the sun came out, and it was summer again, smiling in the winsome loveliness that follows the rain. We packed up, explored the odd corners of quaint Kirkby Lonsdale and then, yielding to an irresistible temptation, returned to the river to spend a luxurious half-hour in the cool water again.

Again I parted from my comrades: this time I continued my ride up Lunesdale, where many a lovable scene lured me into lazy contemplation. Vaguely aware that to approach Sedbergh would take me away from the river, I turned onto a road I had not known before, and it is a fierce mountain road of long steep grades and crinkly mountain views. Above Lowgill (what's in a name!) the Kendal road comes in and then slides down a wild pass to kiss the Lune again and swing upward into Tebay. On that pass I sit even now with low murmurs beside me, and a little wind, a warm zephyr playing around.

Monday 3 pm., 3 miles above Kentmere, July 7th, Another mountain beck!

I have come over Nan Bield. From here the valley-head is enclosed by fine crags; locked up, it seems, beyond access. But there is a way, and I have come that way.

Last night I left you at Tebay. My way was by new and lovely country through Orton to Shap, and a devilish hard way it was. But life is that way and mostly not nearly so pleasant as that toil of a road to Shap. These hard mountain roads knock hunger into you, and if you are without food they take your knee-strength away and leave you gasping inches where you have strode yards of yore, but you learn a lot; you come up again like a cork in a storm and get yourself beached alright. In the dirty toil of that foundry I left a fortnight ago you are punched but you have to go on, and gyrate daily with a destination as viciously circular as the gyrator[4]. You breathe filthy sulphurs from liquid metal alongside of equally filthy rhetoric from your fellow-workers, and the liquid heat of that sooner or later finds a mould in you, corroding you just as the rest of them are rotted. It is a fine thing to get yourself out now and then and let these mountain roads punch the rot away!

At Shap I turned down a little lane I have known before, and before dropping down to Bampton, spent a mental battle over two alternatives, Swindale and Mardale[5]. Mardale won, and in spite of Manchester's attempts to cut up the nature of things, I found Haweswater a winsome sight that evening. I pitched my tent at Mardale – that village doomed in a City Council chamber – the kind of place I shall feel a lump rise in my throat the day the inflating waters of the re-created lake pour over it. There is a tiny grey church there with huge old yews spreading over the churchyard, a sprinkling of stone-built farms with rosy gardens and honeysuckle hedges, and the dale is headed by great crags that will always scotch highway intrusion. A hiker pitched near me, and we chatted the night out – we, a university student on vacation, and an iron-moulder 'on the dole'! It's the game that puts us level and all square with each other, the game we play and fight out!

Fig. 23: Shap Abbey

I'm a lazy camper. This morning I started at 10.30 am., after careful directing by my companion-camper. He did his best to put my mind off Nan Bield, for he had come that way the day before, and he saw I had a cycle, but I had set my heart on it. The Dun Bull Inn, lying below Harter Fell, marks the joint start of Gatesgarth and Nan Bield pass, and

---

4   Foundry process.
5   Mardale is now buried beneath the Haweswater reservoir, but at the planning stage in 1930.

after half a mile or so of stony lane the tracks break in two, the Nan Bield section continuing along the valley for a little way, and the Gatesgarth immediately commencing its zig-zag route to the 1900 odd feet summit. But Nan Bield is very faintly marked, Gatesgarth being well defined, so, in complete forgetfulness of directions, I followed the clearer route.

Twenty minutes later, in a condition of great perspiration I found myself well up the mountainside with Haweswater far below, a fine sheet of water in a fold of the hills, and Mardale at its head in green tranquillity. But I was getting suspicious, and perusal of my map made it clear that I was halfway over Gatesgarth. The crags of Harter Fell lay between the two passes, and I ought to have either gone back to the lane or abandoned thoughts of Nan Bield and crossed Gatesgarth into Sleddale. Instead, with admirable pigheadedness, I determined to risk the crags to keep the altitude I had gained, and in pursuance of that policy, went straight 'at the face' of Harter Fell. Harter Fell may be a rock-climbers paradise, but it was a fool's paradise to me, loaded with a bicycle and full camping kit. For two hours I paraded a mile of fellside, perambulating here and there in avoidance of precipice; scrambling up rocky slopes, scrambling down rocky slopes, struggling, bike on shoulder, to dizzy ridges only to struggle back again, baffled, confused. I trod ledges on the cliffs and missed half a dozen deaths by less inches till my shoulders ached with the strain of the iron cross-bar, my knees were bleeding and my ankles twisted. But I won through! From seeing Smallwater, a rock-bound Tarn half-way over Nan Bield, lying below me like a pear-shaped sheet of glass, I took heart, and needed it too, for I actually had to descend until well below the tarn in order to gain the track I had seen on the western side.

From Smallwater the track soared another thousand feet, and I soared with it, at least as much as anyone laden as I was, can soar on a rocky track. Near the top I met two men, trampers, from Birmingham, and they made a great show of amazement and admiration at my 'feat' (so they called it). They asked why I did it, and my answer was a pointing finger at the mountain grandeur around, Mardale a green cup far below, and Smallwater, dreaming in its rocky fastness. Why indeed? We parted on great terms. Then the summit cairn with the Rock and Fell Club's signpost, 2,100 ft., 'in heaven'. On the other side the aspect was different, moorlands ahead, and Kentmere Valley. The path went down in mazy coils and crooks, often exchanging places with a stream. In the valley I spied a road across a wide moor, leading down from some lead mines, so I forsook my track, spent an energetic period crossing, and so came down to this stream.

My food supplies have gone: my lunch has consisted of a crust of brown bread and a little fruit, and now, after jotting these notes I feel the call of hunger again. Well, I covered six miles in four and a half hours, and if the next six occupy so long the mountains will have knocked my knees away!

Monday night 11 pm., Newby Bridge, July 7th

I write by candle light, camped in a field of new-mown hay. There are scents and warm softness about hay, and I have found the discomforts too. Tiny flies exactly the colour of the hay are jumping and flying everywhere with terrific speed. Hay is everywhere too; I have fished it from the butter and the tea, the milk is full of floating straws, and I constantly find myself eating it.

The farmer and his men are greatly interested in my outfit, and the only payment asked for eggs and milk is a few cigarettes of which they are short. They have worked today from 4.30 am. till after 10 pm., for the weather is glorious and a fine day is promised tomorrow. At the farm the old lady refused to fill my canvas water bucket, incredulous that it will hold water, and I filled it myself to her utter astonishment.

After my belated snack this afternoon I tackled Garburn Pass from Kentmere. Compared to Nan Bield, Garburn shrinks in height, attaining a modest 1,450 ft., but it is a beautiful moorland track traversing rock scenery, turfy grass and bracken, and crossed by cascading streamlets as clear as crystal. The summit of Garburn is a supreme viewpoint, with all the western peaks strung out in rocky grandeur, the Troutbeck valley, and Kirkstone Pass wriggling clear of the enclosing heights like a brown ribbon flung down the mountainsides. On the steep descent to Troutbeck the track was mostly rideable, though sometimes a mere heap of stones, and beyond that pretty little village, on a lane, I obtained an almost full length view of Windermere, counting that view better than any impression that may be gained by riding the shores of the lake. I avoided Ambleside, crossed the head of the lake, and joined Coniston road, where at Skelwith Bridge it climbs, giving a view down Langdale and of the Pikes that must imprint itself on the memory as sheer beauty. Such scenes endear one to the Lakeland country for always. I got the dreaded 'knock' on that climb, and as I was yet breathless, I got my stove going and cooked a great pan of porridge with water, and so cured my complaint.

By Tarn Hows I descended to Coniston and laid in my stores there, then, crossing the head of the lake I joined the lane down the east bank of the lake. More lovely lakeside scenery cannot be conceived than this eastern side of Coniston. There are wooded banks of fir and pine, occasional meadows of soft green, little headlands and bays and wooded knolls where the

Fig. 24: Hawkshead, where Wordsworth lodged, and Newby Bridge

trees are reflected faithfully in the clear water. Across the lake is the Old Man of Coniston, and looking towards the head of the lake the highest giants range themselves like guardians of the inner recesses. Though the evening was tranquillity itself, over the Old Man black storm-clouds gathered with all the portend of a heavy July thunderstorm, and giving a heightened aspect of grandeur to the ranges. The storm did not come my way, and I left the lake at High Nibthwaite still in the peaceful mood of a summer evening. I traversed an intricate network of little lanes till I reached the Barrow-in-Furness road. Near Backbarrow, at the roadside and apparently abandoned was a perfectly reproduced stage coach of the coaching era, and across it was painted 'Deadwood Mail'. In a somewhat ruinous condition, it certainly left a picturesque touch of the past in my mind. Eventually I reached the reedy foot of Windermere at dusk, having crossed head and foot of the lake, and found this site just far enough from the main road for comfort.

At home, Friday, July 11th

This weekend I have my last fling at freedom, for on Tuesday I must return to work. The weather is dry, and so it may be that I have had the best three weeks of the summer. There is little that I may write concerning my return from Newby Bridge on Tuesday. My route was along the swinging highway to Lindale, the flat, wind-hampered trek across the estuary to Levens, and then the main road south with its varying degrees of beauty and its incessant busy hum, culminating in the really fine moorlands which give the lie direct to those who say the approach to Bolton, a Lancashire industrial centre, must necessarily be dull and monotonous.

Chipping, Lancashire, Morning, July 14th 1930

The last day of my liberty! Like a prisoner on ticket of leave I must report myself, and tomorrow I shall be gyrating again in the same unyielding circle that I left on June 23rd. I am feeling regretful.

It was arranged that I meet my two confreres, Fred and Joe, at Horton-in-Ribblesdale at 6.30 pm. last Saturday night. Horton is a Dale-village six miles above Settle where the river is only a noisy youngster, barely six miles long, and a winsome spot withal. It was our intent to camp at Brow Gill Head, of which more anon.

I left home in brilliant sunshine, and crossed the moors to Blackburn, emerging into the Ribble valley, and, facing Blackpool bound traffic from the Yorkshire towns, found escape at last in a little lane to Worston where I had tea. Then I hugged close to Pendle and descended into Downham, one of Lancashire's prettiest villages, made my way to Chatburn to the highway again, and a mile further along, left it again for the quieter way through Bowland Forest, by villages with such names as Wigglesworth and Rathmell to Settle. Again all the joys of summer evening, this time in Ribblesdale, and on a bridge in Horton I met Fred. Whilst awaiting Joe we decided to seek a certain 'perfect' bathing pool on the Ribble, given by a book on Ribblesdale, but though we searched for an hour, being joined by Joe, and located the right spot, the river had sunk to a mere stream too shallow to allow us the semblance of a splash. We continued up the dale, along the hilly road through Selside, and two miles from the junction at Ribblehead turned down a gated track through a farm yard, by a terraced slope and along the valley bottom where the river is merely a stream, to reach Nether Lodge Farm, where we enquired after a campsite. Certainly! Anywhere in all the acres of green fields, and milk in plenty and eggs too! We found a sheltered place by the beck that runs from Ling Ghyll, and there had supper as the sun set, and saw the full moon rise and roll in unclouded brilliance as we turned in, and our music the depleted murmur from Ling Ghyll beck.

Fred had us up early, and by 9 am. we were away, loaded with candles for Brow Gill Cave. On our way we crossed 'God's Bridge', a natural limestone bridge where the stream has worn a way through the rock. Brow Gill stream is very pretty just below the cave, for it has furrowed a tortuous gorge through the rock. The entrance to Brow Gill is the outlet for the beck, and yesterday we found access very simple, for never had the farmer seen the water so low – merely a trickle through the rock.

An uncomfortable feature of Brow Gill Cave is the razor like sharpness of the furrowed rock, which cuts into you like a knife, and in places where the roof is low and progress is only gained by crawling, the knees are apt to become a little butchered, or the head and even the neck suffers, brutally. The first ten yards were a 'doddle', for Brow Gill begins with a lofty arch.

Joe discovered a passage while Fred and I spent a period squirming on our stomachs over wet rock, and we all met on the other side, Joe spick and span, we somewhat slimy. With Fred and I this is certain to happen when we go pot-holing, for, in the nature of things (it seems) the lowest, awkwardest holes are those which go farthest, often leading to caverns of architectural might, and breathless beauty locked in eternal night. The stream had disappeared, sunk in the chaotic floor, and we found a lateral fissure twenty feet high or more, but narrow enough for one to pass at once, and piled up in a confusion of rock. There were no stalactites. A hollow murmur ahead announced the presence of the stream again, and after a little scrambling we entered a great cavern, roughly circular in shape, thirty or forty feet high, and filled with the sound of falling water. As I have stated, the stream was depleted, but coming down in a single fall of perhaps thirty feet, and flanked by a column of yellow stalactite reaching from roof to floor, it made a grand sight, even in the flickering candle light.

Further progress was problematical then, for in the smooth-walled cavern the only possible way was by climbing up the waterfall, a haphazard, dirty business that we preferred to shirk. The difficulty of finding hand and footholds up thirty feet of rock smoothed over by ages of water action is obvious enough, but when the climb must be done in the waterfall and without lights, except a candle below – worse than useless – the difficulty becomes paramount. Turning back, we examined the fissure which gave us access to the cavern, and behind a curtain of rock on the left wall we found a 'staircase'. Do not run away with the notion of a flight of steps! That 'staircase' was a nasty affair of delicate ledges few and far between, and

Fig. 25: Lyth Valley and River Gilpin, Westmoreland

about twenty feet up they ended, necessitating us taking a step across the fissure to the opposite wall, crossing back again when we saw a broad ledge open out across the cavity. Joe remained below on terra firma, and, as I stood astride thirty feet above him and contemplated a slip onto the sharp rock below I almost praised his good sense. When Fred came up we moved along the ledge, and found a labyrinth of tunnels about 18 inches high and quite smooth. Though almost laid down, travel had more comfort, for our bare knees took more kindly to smooth rock. Our candles eventually showed us a parapet, and peeping over, we saw the stream disappear in a white fleck below. We had reached the lip of the waterfall. A hail brought Joe back into the cavern which he illuminated by placing pieces of candle at vantage points, with a romantic effect seen from above.

We clambered over our parapet into the stream and continued our journey, first without difficulty, but as the roof became lower we returned to our kneeling posture with the extra discomfort of the stream. A little further the kneel became a crawl, the crawl a wriggle in the water, and at last we moved in inches flattened out in the stream. Our hopes ceased when roof and water almost met in front.

The worst was not over. As we had moved head first, we must return feet first for some yards. Try it on the rug at home if you think it's easy. Lie down on your stomach, keep your arms pressed to your side and slide backwards round the room. If you can then, imagine a couple of inches of running water under you, and a lumpy wall of rock encasing you, while, at the same time, you strive to keep a lighted candle in!

At last we got clear of the water channel, traversed the tunnels in the roof, and returned to the ledge above the crevice. Joe, from below, directed our descent, which was more difficult than ascent for obvious reasons. Shortly after that we returned to the dazzling brilliance of the outside world after 2 hours, exploring Brow Gill cave as completely as any man can do! 'Pot-holing', when you are not equipped for it, is a nasty, dangerous game! We had a splendid walk on the moors to dry ourselves, for the sun was hot, and the moorland birds, the grouse, the curlew and moorfowl sang in a blue sky. You feel glad on such days to be free like these birds, and after the weird, enclosed beauty of the limestone nether-world, the outer world is wide and expansive. You have seen the marvels of water-worn fissures and caverns; you have endured the discomforts and risked something, and now, safe, you feel like singing and running, or frolicking like a week-old lambkin that has just discovered the sunshine. Your lacerated knees have ceased to smart, your back no longer aches with constant bending; the bumps on your head have miraculously healed themselves and nothing in the whole world matters – not even if you are one of the rejected ones 'on the dole'!

We saw many a deep, unfenced pothole, like Calf Hole with its natural bridge that gives the appearance of a twin pothole, and others un-named, numbered by the Ordnance Survey maps. To descend them was impossible without ropes or rope ladders so we gazed and passed on to talk on widely varied subjects, Socialism, Atheism and matrimony to name but three. A party of three that claimed three adherents to Socialism, three to Republicanism, three opponents to matrimony, and two of us quite convinced Atheists!

Still at Chipping, after lunch, same day

I hate to leave. It has rained all morning, but the sun is struggling through now, and the green world is the fresher for the rain. There is nothing ill about this July drizzle, no mournfulness in the drops that fall from these oak leaves like there often is in Autumn. Summer is in her full glory, and summer in England is a song. Our climate has the moods of a wilful child, but lovely sights and things come of it.

Yesterday we lingered late at Nether Lodge Farm, and would fain have lingered still, for the heart of Ribblesdale is sweet, and the farmer liked to hear from us of the tours and the way the towns are faring. We had to force ourselves away. After tea in the Forest of Bowland, we moved along to Sawley where I bade my comrades good-day, and traced a wavering route along the north bank of the Ribble, through Waddington (a charming place) to Mytton. It was in my mind then to go direct to Chipping, but the rain came, and I found a peculiar pleasure in its company. The rhythm of the tyres and the feel of it beating on the bare head was like a tonic, so I stretched the short ride to Chipping into a great circle round by the moorland fringe at Bashall Eaves, and along the Vale of Chipping to camp at dusk in a heavy downpour.

Conclusion, at home after work, July 16th

For two days I have been in the foundry again. There is dirt and grime and the filth of men's minds there. They did not cross the Derbyshire uplands three weeks ago, from the sweltering dale at Ashford-in-the-Water to Moneyash, Revidge, Flash and Allgreave. They did not know the sense of ease at Mouldsworth Mere in rural Cheshire, the crossing of the Peckforton hills, the delicious loveliness of Nant-y-Ffrith at the moment the silver music of the stream broke into my waking senses.

Today I have wondered if Groes Llwyd, that meadow by the Dee is as peaceful and I have been wistful of it. The Dee is still there, flowing placidly under the sun, and I am not there to swim or to lie half-naked on the banks, to stroll in leisure with my thoughts, to hear the vocal birds and to smoke at sundown.

My mind cannot be bound to the foundry like the gaggered sand I have bound to iron boxes with my labour. The fells have burned themselves – gaggered their brown slopes – into me, and not all this lifting and ramming and casting can move them! In the hour of pause for the noontide meal these men talk of gambling – some of them, in a corner, pour their thoughts and empty their pockets at a pack of cards – or ramble through last nights beerhouse yarns, smutty tales that only men can tell. I am there, and my ears will not shut these things out, but I hear, above them, the murmur of mountain becks, sound I shall not forget. Then sometime I shall be cast off again, and my wheels will wander through Lakeland in a free-ness that moneyed folks and gamblers alike know nothing of.

Just now the falling water in Brow Gill is thundering in silence – for human ears and eyes are away, and above, on the open fellside, the wheeling curlew flings his notes on desert places. I shall go back to Pen-y-Ghent ere many days. The stranglehold of Nature!

* * * * * * * * * * * *

"Life is sweet, brother .... There's day and night,
brother, both sweet things; sun, moon and stars, all sweet,
things; there's likewise a wind on the heath. Life is sweet,
brother ...."

G. Borrow - 'Lavengro'

THE CAMP ON THE PASS.

Camping at an Altitude.

At Wessenden Head.

"Over the heavens, among the stars we slept."

Wessenden is popular with folks from the West Riding woollen towns, those great, sprawling blots across a fair country. Despite the wild proximity of Pennine, there are valleys near the border that are choked with misshapen masses of brick where humans live and work, and often display a persistent desire to spend their short hours of leisure. What strange people, these, who seem never to feel an urge to leave their own doorstep. What poor minds that never ache to see the distant shires, or even to feel the keen air above, the turf beneath their feet on the looming 'hills of home' above their very roofs! What bends their wills to trouser creases, to delicately adorned hats when a pair of neglected shorts and bare heads will serve them better, at a wanderer's game!

Above their heads the brown Pennine stands. The Pennine is no subordinate thing, like the soft green Southern hills are ploughed out into the shapes the farmer makes to suit his purpose. Men scratch scars on Pennine, but they are scratching with penknives on high walls. Men live on their brown steeps, but not by them, and they mould their desired impression on the nature of the man. If you would prove this you only need to go amongst the Pennine men.

But my story is of Wessenden. From the high road that crosses the range between Mossley on the Lancashire side, and Holmfirth in Yorkshire, a sturdy track runs down a deepening ravine to the north. A mile below the windy summit the first of four reservoirs is laid. No scars, no ungrateful blots, these waterworks, for whatever towns may do, their reservoirs are almost always a credit to their taste. If you stand above the highest lake, the scene, looking down the steep-sided valley, will impress you. Those people who leave their towns with rucksacks and hobnailed boots know Wessenden. At weekend many boots pass its trail.

Waterworks, Corporations and campers never get along together. To pitch a tent, however inoffensively, above or by the drinking supply is to bring down a load of furious officials armed with dark threats of 'further action', and cries of 'contamination'. He who would spend a night there must go under cover of darkness, and pack up early, 'silently steal away'.

So, one warm still evening at dusk, my companion and I climbed out of

Linthwaite, a suburb of Huddersfield, into Wessenden valley, intent on breaking the law in letter and spirit, on the Pass above the highest reservoir. The road was uphill and rough, but there were level places along each water-store, for they are terraced one above the other. We chose to walk in that delightful hour, for the end of May is a pleasant time, in the hills. At Wessenden Lodge the road ceases its existence as such, becoming a mere track; the valley closes in, and the last (or first) lake is narrow, hemmed in. That lake was dark without a reflection for night had fallen; the hills had withdrawn themselves. When the lake was below and not the ghost of a light betrayed the presence of habitation, we began to search for a campsite. Our taste is far from fastidious, but exploration of every inch of ground as we proceeded revealed rock, bog-holes, or great, impossible tufts. We drew near to the summit where a wind was growing, when a narrow ravine conveying a trickling stream, broke into the bank on the left. Higher up this beck, we found a place that just held two tents, an awful pitch for waviness and there was a great wedge of rock there, just in the way, but somehow we got down, curled ourselves round where rock or knobbles protruded, and without trouble slipped into the arms of Morpheus.

The next morning portrayed one of those climatic disturbances that has characterised 1931 – a howling wind and grey skies. Before the first wary keeper had made his round we had cooked and eaten breakfast, and were climbing the last few hundred feet to Isle of Skye. Stolen sweets are good..........

On Garburn Pass

On a sulky evening at the end of June my companion and I met in Kendal, and after exhausting our shopping list – and incidentally, our available space, we sought that lovely lane by Burneside to Staveley – a very attractive escape from the orthodox highway that carries a heavy burden of traffic to the shores of Windermere. A garden is a lovesome thing, as someone has said, but at the end of June gardens are near the apex of their lovesomeness. My companion, with feminine exhuberance, spent a long spell of adoration at some delicately pink roses, and I was impressed. Beside the River Kent we had a picnic tea just at the moment that the sun came out, and life went along very sweetly, like the shallow stream below us. There is half the world in having good companionship; I am very fortunate, and enjoyed that more than the hour of 'Flaming June' along the Burneside lane.

The Windermere road bore us scarcely a mile before we took to the lanes again, and climbed up into the hills. This Troutbeck byway, apart from its personal beauty, gives rare views to the fine mountain groups behind Coniston and the Langdales, but that evening a grey mist marched across, all-obliterating – even the sun, after one hour's glory in the day. Another lane, green with disuse, carried us past a reservoir and into the mountains above Troutbeck. A chat with two elderly gentlemen in search of photographs passed another hour, and when we tackled the serious part of Garburn Pass, the time was growing late, and the advancing mists shrouded all things in a universal greyness and quietness about us. We sought a place to pitch our tents, but rock and scrubby moorlands all the way to the summit deterred us. The summit at nearly 1,500 ft. was worse – an exposed expanse of bog and rock, and with the wraiths of vapour curling about us, we commenced the descent of the steep track on the Kentmere side. We were tired, and getting past hunger, but semi-sheer slopes and slabs of rock looming in the mist kept us going, until the track leaped down in an almost complete twist – a hairpin bend round a turfy bank. On this little knoll, bounded on three sides by the path, we found a perfect pitch for two tents. Below us a stream tinkled its crystal course, and across the wild regions climbed into the grey void. Once, for a moment, the mist broke, and from our vantage point the deep valley of Kentmere far below lay revealed. Then all was blank, and we turned in. Thirteen hundred feet above the sea.

At about 2.30 I awoke and looked out. It was not night, but impenetrable mingling of mist and darkness at the very tent. Not a sound....... Not the sight of one's own guideline....... I sank back into slumber immediately.

Voices awoke me; some early hikers on the path. I called to my companion, and jumped out. The sun was shining in a blue sky, and only a wisp of mist slid across the peaks over the stream. Below, Kentmere lay in its patterned fields, and across the mountain ridge cut the dappled splendour of the sky. The stream was cold, invigorating to hands and face. At breakfast we watched the farmers with their dogs starting on the annual round of the sheep; shearing time is here.

In country like this, tents and all one's personal belongings can be safely left for hours without the fear of interference, for the type of people who covet the property of others never get in these places. We left our outfits and took a long tramp over the fells – on the breezy summits of Saletarn Knotts, where the views extended far over the Lakeland monsters. I know of few greater joys than to sit on some rocky knoll and trace the windings of roads and stream far below, and see the varied colours in the fields; wheat, oats, clover meadows and pastures. As we descended we came into view of the tents, tiny white specks in a brown and black ravine, bravely perched on their little green ledge!

At lunch-time the farmers came down, spread out, with their dogs guiding sheep towards the pens three hundred feet below us. The mountains awoke to the lusty calls; echoed the plaintive cries of herded sheep: only the lithe dogs worked quietly, swiftly.

That was the camp on Garburn Pass.

Cefn-yr-Odfa

On a day in mid-May, 1929, Fred and I hastened our own ways to a most unorthodox meeting place. I found him hunched up under his cape striving to win shelter from the wind and rain beside a dilapidated gate-post. I would expect nobody else there, for the position was on Ce-fn-hir-Fynydd, 1,374 ft., at a lonely cross-tracks above Llanarmon DC. The outlook promised nothing; just grey banks of drizzle drifting on the Ber-wyns, bringing premature dusk. Down below in Glyn valley there was no rain – on the Cheshire plains that I had crossed there had been sunshine, but these changes were never surprises, for Fred and I had grown used to them.

Fig. 26: A Typical Cheshire inn

Fred hailed me, and spoke of camping. We were both tired after seventy miles with a mornings work as well behind us, and there had been a head-wind from the south-west. We tramped down a wet track beside a thick forest of pine, and shortly dipped down sixty feet to a stream meandering through a marsh of rushes. The track wormed up again to a drizzly skyline, and we were tired.......... We pitched the one tent in a place by the marsh where only one tent would go. Not marshy, but not dry, and the long guide in front was the bog. There were slugs, or black snails, about, but we turned in and went to sleep with heavy scent of the pine forest in our nostrils, and the tattoo of the rain on the tent in our ears.

A whaup [sic] awoke us, calling overhead. The rain had ceased, and above the rushes the stream was no worse than brown from the peat. Unsuspicious rabbits abounded; a gorgeous plumed pheasant awoke the dark silence of the forest, and the sheep with frolicksome lambs passed the tent. The time was 7.30. We breakfasted while the tent dried, then packed up and continued our journey. On the skyline, reached by the track at 1,432 ft., we saw the great sweep of the Berwyns we meant to cross, and on them grey banks of drizzle drifted from the southwest.

We dipped down to the narrow burn of the Iwrch, and our campsite below Cefn-yr-Odfa was lost to sight, as events proved, for another year.

Cwm-y-Rhynwedd

There had been a glorious sunset of shooting colours, and, as Fred and I rode along the level valley between Mold and Denbigh, we regretted that we had no better vantage point. With better luck we would have been on the heights in time, but a little, awkward breeze had snapped our time away at every bend. The street lamps of Denbigh were winking in the dusk when we walked leisurely up the long hill that constitutes one of the main streets. High jinks permeated the town – carnival streamers; flags of the nations that we were allied to in the War; pretty girls in scanty but attractive attire, and men absurdly made up, cadging the passers-by with collection boxes. Who ever saw a carnival that did not carry a legion of such, which make a convivial affair into a business and a nuisance! The words "God Save the King", blazoned across the street reminded us that this day was Empire Day, and we fell into a fit of remorse because we had forgotten to tie our

Fig. 27: A Glorious Sunset

little Union Jacks to our bikes. Let it be known that one town in Britain is faithful to its sovereign and the Empire, for does not patriotism consist in the number of flags that are waved, and the number of fervent slogans spread about the streets, on this one blessed day of the year. For the true meaning of Empire Day you must go to Denbigh. Shades of Owen Glyndwr!

Happily Denbigh is small. We began the heavy climb on the Pentre Foelas road, and with darkness drawing a black curtain over all things, climbed to meet a gale. Those long, gradual slopes that cover most of the 8 miles to the summit became un-rideable. Bylchau – 'The Passes' – with its chapel and pub, and its two or three cottages all stuck a thousand feet up on a ridge, began the untamed moorlands, whose dark heights we could not see, but where the wind bore rain across to us. We could find no campsite, no sheltered place of smooth turf, and pushed forward until a dimly lighted farm below the road gave us the last hope. The summit was only a hundred yards above us, with its long miles of successive bogs, exposed to the whims of the night.

The farmer was a kindly man, and made us welcome. His holding was small, a single poor pasture wrested from the wilds, dipping down at one end into a marsh, but with a storm-lantern he showed us the way, and we pitched in the best place on that unsheltered space. Milk and eggs he gave us too, refusing money, which, however, was passed on to the ragged children, whose delight was alone worth the few coppers.

During a slow, comfortable supper, the rain came and went in fierce storms; the tents shook with the force of the wind, and from a single tree beside the farm came burdened creaks and groans. Consciousness of these things soon disappeared as the warm cosyness of sleeping bags stole across us.

We awoke in a beating rainstorm at 7 am. Our plans were for a far thrust into Merioneth, so resisting the temptation to 'turn over', we rushed off to the nearby stream for a hurried wash, and then settled down to breakfast. The rain ceased once; the wind swept the clouds away, and a magical scene of mountain vales, woods and lowlands lay before us, bounded by the silver line of the sea! Then the rain came down again. We packed up in the rain; at 9 am. we moved off – in the rain – and reached the windswept summit. Whilst we rode the rain was pushed aside, and all the splendid giants of Shire-Carnarvon appeared on the far horizon. One more shower at Pentre Foelas was the last that day. The sun and a freckled sky with following winds will make that day stand out. A night at 1,500 ft. and a morning over

Fig. 28: The Cromlech, Llanberis Pass

the Denbigh moors; into Cwm Penmachno; up the grassy Bwlch to Rhaiadr Cwm; across Arenig to the Tryweryn and down to Bala and a fast run home is only an outline of a fact that was finely set out in colour tones, and retains its shading in our memory.

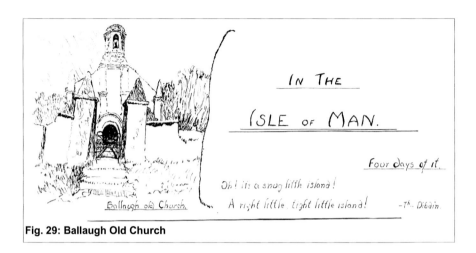

In The

Isle of Man.

Four days of it.

Oh! its a snug little island!
A right little, tight little island! — Th. Dibdin.

Ballaugh old Church.

Fig. 29: Ballaugh Old Church

September had reached its wetter and colder half when I found myself toying with the idea of a long weekend before Winter proper set in and brought the end of camping. The worst of weekends is that they are never long enough, even when extended from Friday until Tuesday. In that year of grace, 1930, many erstwhile two-day trips had been stretched into double that time, and my pocket as well as my employer had suffered in consequence. The material result was an alarming slump in financial status and industrial confidence, but neither of those caused me half so much concern as would the frustration of one weekend. Such is my material debasement. Mentally I felt as though the intellectuals were near me, and were it not for my sheer neglect of study and things classical, I sometimes thought I might aspire to some lowly pinnacle of knowledge.

How all this would end I knew not, and cared less. When youth leaves my side I shall be speedily relegated to that industrial scrap-heap which is the abiding fear of nearly all working-class men of middle age, unless I pull myself up, and descend to that state of highly respectable humbug which is assiduously practised by most people. I think I prefer to drift on as I am, and, as one eminent political irresponsible has said: *"damn the consequences"*.

I like to think that I have a fairly strong streak of the nomad in me. If you are inclined to ask why I <u>like</u> to think so, I shall answer that I <u>like</u> to think of it, and that is enough for me. Maybe I shall finish life as a nomad; I'd far rather do that than pass my days behind a bare wall of respect and convention, working a tortuous eight and a half hours a day, visiting equally tortuous friends and relatives o'nights, and wasting precious Sundays swallowing the haberdashery of professional religionists, and chanting silly recantations to a very problematical God. The fools – spending so much time and energy in pursuit of an improbable future state, while the only world they are sure of, is waiting for them to enjoy it, to make it worth living in.

The idea of a weekend in the Isle of Man grew upon me. Weekend excursions at cheap fares are issued by the steamship company, and I resolved to take advantage on the last weekend they were available, the second in September. Thus I left home at 9 pm. on the Friday evening, to catch the midnight boat from Fleetwood. The ride by night was eventless and pleasant, for the night was placid, moonlit, and devoid of traffic, and I boarded the new, one-class boat 'Lady of Man' with half an hour to spare.

On the 'Lady of Man' berths are free, taking the form of long couches in tiers of two at various points on the ship. I chose an upper berth in the warmest part of the ship, composing myself to sleep. The impossibility of this became apparent when an invasion took place, possibly from a railway train, and all the tables in the room became occupied. The reason for this large, impatient company became obvious when, as the ship got under way, a bar opened directly opposite me, and soon Babel reigned. Although I was sleepy and sleepless most of the way, the great interest I drew from studying the people who drank the night hours away kept me from boredom. Even drink palls, for when the engines ceased, and the bar closed, there was a bleary-eyed silence all around.

The boat arrived at 5 am. and I was soon making my way to Douglas promenade. The prom was hardly astir, darkly lit, and cold. It was not my first visit, though there is a vast difference between visiting Douglas for a holiday and visiting the Isle of Man with cycle and camping kit. I had resolved first to follow the coast until I reached Douglas again, and I soon began to put it into effect by climbing Onchan Head, not by the road, but by a footpath from Derby Castle by the Port Jack Camp to Port Jack, a fine little bay with a good bathing place. While I had lunch there, dawn broke, and the sea became gradually

Fig. 30: Ride by Night

suffused with light. A fine bit of coast scenery, and the path among rock and bramble – difficult to drag the bike along – showing the bay to the best advantage. My wanderings took me to a deep ravine on the coast, blocked up by a high concrete wall, on the top of which a path was made and protected by railings. A series of iron ladders led down into the depths of the gorge which gave off a strong scent of brine. I had half decided to descend to the bed of it and investigate the reason for this great prison, when a man with a uniform came up, bad me 'good morning', and with a sack over his shoulder, went down. Reaching the bottom, he entered a small cave at the side, and shortly after came back with his sack empty. He had been feeding something, it was clear, though what it was I knew not. I afterwards found out that this deep gorge was used as a bear pit, and was glad I had not personally investigated. A bear, confined like that one, is not an amenable animal.

I reached a road again, and by the coast enjoyed really fine rock scenery to Groudle Glen, at the mouth of which I picked out a rough lane which soared up behind the cliffs. I was tired then, from a day's work and a sleepless night, and obtained ready consent to camp for a few hours in a field by a cottage. So I pitched before 8 am. and slept soundly until half past one in the afternoon. The weather had broken: a heavy mist, full of rain, drove in from the sea, and I packed up in a storm. The lane passed the ruins of St Lonan's church, then a branch swung out by Clay Head, though the rain took the views away. At Garwick Bay I struck the main road to Laxey, where a steep lane led me down to Old Laxey, with its quaint harbour at the river mouth, and closely packed houses. The wind and the rain played fury there, but it was great to stand at the seaward wall and look over Laxey Bay at the half-obscured cliffs of Clay Head. I crossed the bridge, climbed steeply, and joined the highway by the electric tramway, where both climb together by the side of Sliean Ouyr, 1,483 ft., and again give lovely seaward views. I came to Dhoon Glen hotel, paid my threepence, and inside the cape, walked down the Glen.

In June, July and August, I can imagine Dhoon Glen to be a show-place almost always crowded with holiday makers on a trip from Douglas. There are many seats placed on vantage points, where, throughout the summer days people will sit and rest, eating chocolates, sandwiches, smoking cigarettes, and throwing paper about. The kind of people who usually spend their holiday at Douglas contain a great proportion of those whose regard for natural beauty is set at a low standard, and they go to Dhoon Glen and such places only because it is a welcome break in the journey by electric tramway to Ramsey. If the summer happens to be dry or just ordinary, the

Glen will be pretty. But when I walked slowly along the well-kept path down to the sea, the rain had swollen the stream, and the leaves were falling. Isle of Man gets an early Autumn. Dhoon Glen was lovely, and the waterfall that races and plunges in channels, in leaps, and in broken ropes of white, was as magnificent as most of the North Wales show-falls at their best. That such a small island can muster such a flow of water in a few miles speaks well for the quality of Manx rain. Where the Glen comes down to the sea is like a gorge, and the coastline there surprised me by its grandeur. In a few hours the sea had become storm-tossed.

Soon after retracing my steps, the highway offered me two alternatives, of which I chose the seaward, and came to Glen Mona, which winds for over four miles to the sea, and contains a waterfall. I did not traverse the whole length of the glen, owing to the very wet and long nature of the footpath (a ten-mile walk would have been involved), but assiduously followed a narrow, evil-surfaced lane along the top of the glen, with, at whiles, glimpses of wooded ravine and grey sea, and a backward aspect of mist-soaked moorlands. My effort to hug the coast was spoiled when the lane took a full sweep back to the main road, near Christ Church. I crossed Glen Corony, and found another lane no better, that descended to the beautiful little hamlet called Cornah, built of stone with luxuriant gardens house-high. There I paid a visit on foot to Ballaglass Falls, a wide cascade of three parts, not great or big, but of good effect. The wet weather was making each fall a spectacular display.

At Cornah, I was not more than 18 miles from Douglas, but such was the nature of the varied attempts to see the coast and the best the glens could offer, that the time was now 5 pm. I had left Douglas 12 hours before. While I ate tea by the wayside above the hamlet, the rain ceased, and I was able to put my cape away. Still faithfully seeking the sea by the aid of my 'halfinch map', I joined a rocky road by the farm of Ballafayle to Bally-garry, a bleak little hamlet, and so reached Maughold. Maughold is quaint, possessing a sundial and Saxon cross of antiquity. But greater is the headland reached by a short path – 300 ft. cliffs down to the sea, and a rugged coastline, headlands and promontories at the foot of which the spindrift whirled and the breakers rolled white-capped. In truth I had fallen in love with Manxland!

Two miles beyond Maughold, the earth suddenly fell away before me. Ramsey was below, on the edge of level pastures, and a golden strip of sand edged the great sweep of the bay. From Tableland Point I descended into the second town of the Island, and stayed there just long enough to lay my stock in for the night. I never saw the promenade, but passed through along

Fig. 31: Maughold

a road as flat as the last ones had been hilly. As I rode nearest the coast, the sun came out, and I could see the sea glittering on my right. When the road took a twist away from the coast, I turned along the first lane, and then became involved in a network of treacly marsh-lanes that finally ended at a gate. Not two hundred yards away I could see a road and people passing to and fro, but such an area of the bog lay between that I turned back and made my way through laborious mud to the small compact village of Bride. A heap of stones called a road took me along a dreary, windy level to the sea and the single farm grandly termed Port Cranstal. The lighthouse on Point of Ayre was only a mile or so away, but there was no attraction in the ride, so I turned back to Bride and took the Jurby road along Glentruan, which is not a glen at all, but only a name. The Jurby road is quite level and of excellent surface; moreover the scenery is rural with that strange air about it that makes it not English.

Dusk was creeping up, and the last traces of the day's rain still hung over the hills. The glory of that rural road to Jurby is in the views of the hills. The mist lent them remarkable grandeur. At one time I was startled into a belief that I was really looking across the lowlands to snow-puffed alps and glacial rivers; at another I could easily imagine myself gazing into the mysterious highlands when the grey mists boil up from the glens to lend their shrouding grandeur to those heathery island hills. I hardly saw the sea, but a furlong away on the north side of the road, yellow dunes betrayed the end of the land, and there were houses on that near horizon, sometimes spaced at lonely intervals of half a mile, sometimes clustered into hamlets like Ballall, Cronkbreck and Sartfield.

A mile beyond tiny Jurby, the Carlane River runs under the road and enters the sea. A sandy track beside the stream went past two houses to the shore, and along that track I passed at dusk. I was very fortunate to chance that way, for behind a sheltering dune, but with the tide at my feet, I discovered a perfect stretch of turf, and pitched my tent there.

Can you conceive of a pleasanter thing than to camp within sound of the sea, to cook your supper as you look out across darkening waters, and to go to sleep as your ears make music from the splash of sea-waves!

The tide was up. As I lay half-awake, I could hear it, pounding on the shore, not six yards away. The strong tang of ocean was on my lips – my face had a pleasing smart. With my bathing costume, I jumped out and saw the sea there, restless and reflective, laid out to a dim horizon where sea and sky joined, and not the bare shadow of earth to break the ocean plain. The sea was cold – exhilarating for a quick splash and out again – to breakfast.

At 9 am. I was on the road again, hugging the coast as much as I could, though the road turned inland for a time to Ballaugh, with its old church of the type particularly Manx, and its bridge made notorious by the 'TT' motorcycle races. At Ballaugh I came onto the TT course, a broad highway, and pleasantly quiet that morning, running towards the coast again to Kirk Michael, where the course turns away into the hills. From Kirk Michael to Peel, the road abounds in seaward views, running almost along the coast, which itself is neither sandy nor rocky, but quite good to eyes that love the places where land and ocean meet.

Peel is a show-place. If you have not been to Peel, you have not seen the Isle of Man: if you have been to Peel you have – to argue in the same

Fig. 32: Peel

strain. If you have been to Peel, you went on St Patrick's Isle to the Castle, listening to, and looking at, mummified history touched up with pretty legends. The day I was at Peel the show had ended for the summer, and though a cool pleasant breeze blew, people wrapped themselves up as they walked the half-deserted promenade. I didn't go to the Castle; didn't even set foot upon the 'Blessed Isle of Patrick', but the docks, wherein flows the little Neb stream, were interesting, and smacked of fishing. My road negotiated narrow streets, and then went round the back of Contrary Head, where someone has stuck a monument and called it Corrin's Folly, presumably because one Corrin was foolish enough to build up there for no reason whatever. I can record countless cases about people credited with good sense doing things daily that put Mr Corrin's folly in the shade.

A dip and a nasty bend nearly precipitated me into Glen Maye, but my brakes are good, and I paid tuppence to walk down. Glen Maye has an attracting name, and it attracts worthily. This side of the island is facing east, so, naturally, this is the colder side, and already the woods are faintly brown. The waterfall in Glen Maye was in spate – one grand leap, as though the flood was determined to make my tuppence worth while. As in Dhoon Glen, the stream enters the sea by a fine little gorge at a point called in Manx 'Traie Cronkan', where a good stretch of the rocky Contrary Head is visible. At Glen Maye Hotel I had seen a magnificent car drawn up with a chauffeur within dressed faultlessly. Halfway down the Glen I met what I guessed to be the possessors of the car. Incongruous is the word for that party. A stout lady dressed in expensive clothing was panting along under a load of furs in a manner that reminded me of the early days of motorcars. With her came a painted doll, bejewelled and mortally afraid of speckling her shoes with Glen Maye mud; an elderly man Bond Street tailored to a collar so deep that his chin had a permanent tilt, and a young blood of the Dandy class, who gave me an unsolicited glance of such hauteur, as to make me long to punch him well and truly under his lifted chin. They seemed utterly out of place in Glen Maye.

I climbed uphill, just as the sun broke out and the sea shone as if polished. At Dalby, a long, straight lane led towards the coast, and down it I went to have my lunch by the shore. The road ended dead on the beach at two white-washed cottages. Magnificent! Niarbyl Bay is the greatest bit of coast in all the Isle of Man. There was a coastline worthy of a mighty nation, a rugged series of headlands, one behind the other, of wild solitudes where the gulls swoop and soar and scream to each other, and no other sound is heard but the ceaseless boom of ocean breakers battering creeks and coves in the tall cliffs, and gurgling in long caves. I couldn't leave the

Niarbyl for a long time; I had lunch there; I played about on the rocks: I sat down and dreamed out across the sunny waters; I collected pretty shells and threw them away again. I walked back slowly up the steep road, with many a backward glance. There was no way along the cliffs, so I had to return to the main road. Just as I emerged, two figures came up in cycling clothes, and I recognised them as two of the Bolton CTC. There was the usual surprise on both sides, a long talk, and I gleaned the information that they were camping at The Niarbyl.

Immediately we separated, I plunged down another steep lane to a farm in a glen, across a ford, and up again. The sun got hot, the climb was steep and heavy on a track that grew dense nettles. I was nettled on my bare knee till the blisters rose like the gradient, until I reached a height of 1,189 ft. The sea was far below – across I made out the Irish Coast quite clearly (the Mourne Mountains), and to the north the Scottish coast at Stranraer was visible. Three countries, to include the Island! I passed round the back of Cronk-ny-Iray Llaa, which, on the far side falls an almost sheer cliff of 1,449 ft. to Niarbyl Bay. At the summit another track joined, and the two proved somewhat better together than they had been separately. Rolling moorlands inland changed to sweeping fields of green, and as I reached The Stack, the whole foot of the Island lay out below like a map, the tongue of land to the Calf, with the sea on each side, and Port St Mary and Castletown model places beside a deep-blue sea. Surely, there is nothing dull on the Manx coast!

A steep descent and a puzzling set of roads took me into Port Erin. If I wished to spend a holiday in a seaside resort, I should go to a place like Port Erin. If this place wishes to expand, the growth will have to be at the back of the town, for the two headlands, on each side of the town, effectively block the way. The town is not blatant like so many resorts; neither is it too pretentious, but snug in its deep bay, with Bradda Head, a magnificent headland to the north, and Kione-ny-Garee, rugged and rocky at the southern end. I stood on the stone jetty, watching the bathers and longing to join them. My 'lightweight' costume was insufficient to fulfil the rather strict conditions laid down for sea bathing at towns. As the day was Sunday, I missed my opportunity to visit the aquarium and fish hatcheries, which, controlled by the Manx Fisheries Board, are, I believe, well worth seeing.

From Port Erin (I was still assiduously following the coast) I joined a path leading uphill onto some rolling, down-like moorlands. There was a Druids Circle near the path, and a little beyond was a refreshment hut. To my dismay I discovered that I had only a little brown bread left, as I had made the mistake of neglecting to buy sufficient on Saturday. Sunday is a dead-letter day on the Island. I bought my tea, saving my meagre stock for the morrow's breakfast, and afterwards joined a branch path going right. Further along there were stiles and gates, and then the path reached St Patrick's Footprint. A slab of rock had a concrete box arrangement cemented to it. On top of the box was a spy-glass, and by paying a penny into a slot an electric bulb inside was lighted. Then, I suppose, St Patrick's Footprint comes into view. I surmise the 'footprint' is the shape of a foot water-worn in the rock. All around are outcrops where water has worn hollows. I didn't fall for this absurd catch-penny, which seems to be about the limit in trading on those people whose religion has made ready to swallow any old yarn, so long as it is associated with the saints, or heaven.

Soon after I reached the edge of the cliffs. My pen is inadequate to the task of describing my walk by Aldrick Bay to the Calf Sound on that perfect September evening. The varied beauty of recurring cliff scenery kept me in constant enjoyment, and when I came to the waters-edge at Calf Sound, and saw the tide racing past the two tiny islets of Kitterlan, and through the narrow channel, I just stuck there, as I had done earlier in the day at Niarbyl Bay. The Calf of Man, that great lump of rock, barren and deserted except for a lighthouse and a hut, is an easy swim from the mainland; so close, indeed, that a notice board placed on its shore warning people that it is private property, is clearly readable. As I could not proceed by the coast, I had to turn inland on the one road from Port St Mary for a mile to the exposed hamlet of Cregneish, from where a grass track goes seaward again. I came to the edge of the tall sea-cliffs again at 'The Chasms'; paid tuppence, and was allowed to see the natural curiosities. 'The Chasms' are many great fissures where the sea and natural erosion has found the softest places in the rock. Here the cliffs are 400 ft., so it will be realised how deep some of these narrow, lateral fissures are. From 'The Chasms' I could see Spanish Head, a fine promontory, where, I believe, a ship was wrecked, and still lies at the mercy of the elements. But the finest thing I saw at 'The Chasms' was a gorgeous sunset, slowly diffusing sea and sky in a crimson glow. Crimson to amber, and, as it sank below the horizon, the fan-spread colour in the sky melted and withdrew, as also withdrew the long red track along the smooth waters.

I dawdled past the great cone shaped 'Sugar Loaf' rock stuck out of the sea, by 'Fairy Cave' and the serried headland called Kione-y-Ghoggan to Perwick Bay and Port St Mary, with its quaint old town and its modern one. Port Erin is more in my line. Here the coast flattens out at Chapel Bay, a small bay within the greater sweep of Poolvash Bay, and the road hugs the water's edge to Poolvash Hamlet. Dusk had set in; I left the road (which here turns inland), and kept to a cart-track along the shingle to a farm, where the sole occupant was an ill-behaved dog who set up a protracted howling. The track ended, so I had to turn back, heading inland across the rear of Scarlet Point to Castletown in the dark. A sea-side road runs back to Scarlet; along it I went, searching for a campsite, which would have to be a farm, as this part is flat, populous, and waterless. I found a dilapidated place near the water's edge, where everyone was out, but a passer-by advised me to wait. I waited till 11.30, till the night air came cold across the sea, before anyone turned up. I was fixed up at length – for the story of how, see my short story 'Camping Cameos 5 – The Bull'.

The next morning I was up betimes, and away quite early, to take advantage of this last full day in the Island. The weather was dull and windless; the warm air seemed to be wanting a breeze, and a yacht in the sandy bay lay with sail drooping, that, too, expectant of wind. In the harbour ships were crowded, amongst them two steam packet boats come to rest the winter, their season of traffic and conviviality over for half a year. Over the narrow harbour the grey walls of Castle Rushen stood, the only thing unchanged after centuries of ships. I was struck by a large sign bearing the words 'Herring Manufacturies' in a crowded street. Until then, in my landlubbers profound ignorance, I had believed that herring was a fish that grew in the sea, but now I perceived it to be manufactured by man. Had I not seen the very place it is made? Pondering on this new discovery, I hugged the coast, and then, crossing a flat strip of land (the isthmus called Langness which projects into the sea like a foot), I came to Derby Haven, a meagre-sized hamlet on a cupped bay, sand-choked and reefed at the out-tide. At the edge of the bay, near two houses called Ronaldsway, the road abruptly turns inland to Ballasalla. A footpath hugs the dunes along the foreshore, and as my map promised a through way, I took to the path. The coast began to take on a rugged appearance; with cornfields and barley crops up to the edge of my path, which in turn came near the cliff-edge, I proceeded, stiles and gates at every field barring free travel. Then came a point of beauty, the coast assumed tall cliffs lapped by the gentle waves, and quite suddenly I came to the edge of a sheer-sided gorge, at the bottom of which rushed a stream. Higher up there were woods, ravine-setted, lower downstream the cliffs came to the water, and by the sea a strand of silver sand sloped gently into the green. The cliffs on the coast across the ravine were a hundred feet tall, indented with many caves, fissures and detached rocks of fantastic shapes stood in the tide. The name of the place was like music, Gaelic, perhaps, with a touch of the old pibroch……. Cass-na-Awen…..

does it not linger at the edge of the tongue, like the pibroch lingered in the windy halls of Vaternish?

A hundred yards above the mouth of the ravine, I left the bike and scrambled down with difficulty. It was in my mind to swim, for not a soul was within sight, and as if to urge me on the sun sent golden warmth down. Where a ledge hung over green depths I dived, down to still waters where green weed hung as if in mid-waters. The sudden cold of it shot through me like electricity; colder seas I had never felt, but there was a strength and energy to be drawn from it, and long strokes took me through deep waters into a cave where the light was tinted green from the filtering of the sea. With a swift drying, I went about an exploration with the leisure of a long day before me, and when I climbed back to my bike, I hesitated to leave that lonely, lovely valley. Half a mile higher the ravine had assumed a green gentleness, and my path crossed it. There was a farm there where strangers are unusual, for the kiddies came running out in excitement, and the woman stared and smiled. A green-turfed lane led me over a hill with one glimpse of the sea, and joined the road to Douglas. In half a mile I paid for an excursion down a glen to Port Grenaugh, where people bathed and sat on the rocks, and where a modern café on the sea-edge captured wireless waves and dispelled their music across the gentle sea-waves. The Douglas road was undulating, with little to see, but quiet enough for three miles or more, when, at a toll-gate I was invited to ride around the Marine Drive for 3d., which I paid and swooped down a white road to a tramway line, where cliffs fell down to a lazy sea, and Port Soderick's commercialism, a little hoarse at the season-end, sprawled itself half-a-mile below at the sea-edge. I turned away, along the Marine Drive. The road surface was atrocious, but there is some wonderful engineering about the Drive, which is hewn out of solid rock for many miles, and is fairly well graded. Below, 300 ft., the sea washes the cliff-foot; ever-changing views round headlands, coves (where the road takes great twists and crossed bridges of tremendous height), or out to the open, where the sun shone and all was a-glisten. There is a headland called Little Ness, where the rocks jut out in ugly teeth, coves like Horses Cap, Nuns Choir, Pigeon Cove, and every high-span bridge bears a fanciful name. Finally, Douglas asserts itself, with blatant signs, and as the road falls to the Old Town, the road is full of booths to catch the coins of visitors.

Crossing the bridge into Douglas proper, I provisioned at a confectionery shop, and immediately joined the Peel Road, for little more than a mile took me to Kirk Braddan, where a road right began to climb towards the hills. At this point I had completed the full circuit of the Island, following the coast by road and path as closely as it was possible for me to go with a bicycle. Now it was my intention to do as much of the mountainous inland as possible without re-traversing the same road. In a quiet field I lunched magnificently, then pushed on, constantly uphill into the glen of the river Glass. As I mounted higher, another phase in the variety of this compact little island began to show itself. Pine-trees, great moorland slopes with heather a-bloom, and little ravines contributing cascading streamlets to the clear river, itself little more than a stream. The Baldwin reservoir, Douglas's water supply lies wedged high in the glen; thereafter the road seems to lose its caste, becoming steep, rough and un-hedged. Injebreck river, a stream-let, and wild moorlands, up, up, till it joins the high-road near Snaefell at 1,303 ft. The high road is well surfaced though gated, climbing to 1,406 ft., from where I saw the Island stretched below on three sides, and made out the coast-hills of two lands, Ireland and Scotland, far across a shining sea. On the fourth side Snaefell mountain itself rose like a blister, blocking the view. There is an hotel on Snaefell summit, and a railway line all the way up. I could see the trams like yellow worms crawling up the brown slope and the dark, tiny patches of humanity on the summit. No doubt the view from Snaefell on a clear day is magnificent; no doubt the tramway is a boon to decrepit old gentlemen and invalid old ladies, but as I approached the Sulby fork-road, near where the line passes, I saw a tram with half a load of people who ought to be revelling in the use of their legs and sweet atmo-sphere out of town. Though I could have climbed the extra 600 ft. of Snae-fell in less than half an hour, I preferred to leave it to the trams and hotel-people.

I drifted down Sulby Pass instead. First steep and rough, Sulby Pass is as glorious a stretch of wine-red 'col' as any in our Yorkshire and Derby-shire of the mainland. Below the Pass the winding road down Sulby Glen was heavy with foliage, and cottages nestled where there was room in the narrows. At Sulby, on the Lowlands again, I sprinted along the TT course to Ballaugh, and the Peel road of yesterday again, having tea by a sparkling stream in Bishops Court. The Tourist Trophy Course, ready laid out for the morrow's Senior event, was beribboned and be-posted. The thought struck me that I would have to fix my camp tonight in such a position as to make Douglas accessible in time for the afternoon boat next day. As the road that rings the northern half of the Island is closed to public use while the race is on, it behoved me to make for the southern half, the better to allow me fur-ther exploration to the limit of my available time. Accordingly I made for Kirk Michael, and still continuing along the marked road, turned up Glen Wyllin onto the higher ground, semi-moorland, fringing Sartfell. The road

was quiet with sea-views and an undulating roll like our fellside roads
about the Lune. From a summit at St John's Chapel, I began to descend a
beautiful glen called Craig Wylly's Hill. Dusk was coming when I reached
the elaborate hotel at the entrance to Glen Helen. I had heard much of Glen
Helen, so I decided to see it for myself, paid the entrance fee, and entered. I
walked sharply in the dusk, along a deserted footpath that steadily climbed
through deep woods to Dhenas Fall. By that time the light had almost gone,
and the fall hung like a white fleck down the dark recess of the rock. Another path down the Glen beside the river was not so well kept, and in
places I had some difficulty. By the time I reached the road the hotel was a
blaze of light, sounds of merriment coming from within.

I lit my lamp and pushed on, intent on getting south of this race-course
with its coming racket and crowds, passing a large camp of motor-cyclists,
and reaching St John's, where I bought 'in' at a tiny grocery store, and,
crossing the TT road, climbed steadily up Foxdale. At the cottages of Bal-
lahig, I enquired for a campsite, by a stroke of luck meeting a farmer just as
I was about to seek his place. I obtained ready permission, choosing a
sheltered and cosy spot by the river. Of my subsequent wanderings in pitch
darkness I have already written.[6]

My awakening on this Tuesday morning was hastened by the twin
sounds of rain and motorcycles. Apparently the distance was not far
enough. I went up to the farm for milk and eggs, and settled down to a leisurely breakfast, whilst the rain came in a hard drizzle, and the aspect was
thoroughly hopeless as far as clearing up was concerned.

The thrill of the race half a mile away was without interest to me; I
packed up still in driving rain, and climbed to Foxdale, a mining village
where derelict buildings spoke plainly of trade now departed for ever. From
Foxdale mines I tangled myself in a maze of hilly lanes, white with mud,
through tiny one-house hamlets like Renshelt, Braad and Cloughbane. At a
place called Cooil, a short walk from the old Kirk Braddan, and no more
than three miles from Douglas, I had tea in a cottage attached to a rather
weary-looking mill. In the tiny parlour swarmed myriads of big flies, turning me from my food. However roughly and simply campers live, they de-
mand some measure of cleanliness. At 1.30 pm. I departed in a fury of rain,
making my way to Douglas, and embarking of the Fleetwood boat, due out
at 3 pm.

Thus ended a four day trip to the Isle of Man. I had gone there expecting
to find commercialism over-running natural beauty, as weeds over-run a
hearty crop, and I received a pleasant surprise. Commercialism is rife, no

---

6   Camping Cameos, 'Lost' - to be published.

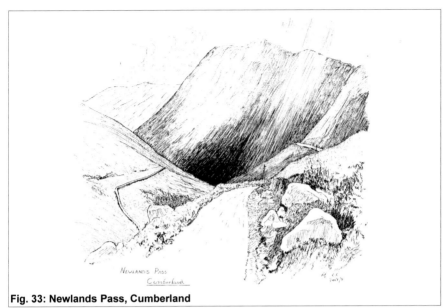

Fig. 33: Newlands Pass, Cumberland

doubt, when the season is at its height, though even the spots can be found where the trippers never go. Isle of Man has gained its name by a certain type of holiday-maker. That same type may have saved it from complete eclipse, by its own bone-laziness. Places like Jurby, where the coast is quiet, The Niarbyl and the Calf of Man are too inaccessible for those people. Cass-na-Awen, I am sure, has never changed since the days when the Isle of Man was only served by a once a week boat, Injebreck is too toilsome a climb for these people, and the glens, though popular, have to be paid for. In September the Isle of Man is lovely and almost lonesome.

The rain never ceased that day. When the slow negotiation of the Lune deep and the sand-banked channel had been accomplished, we berthed at Fleetwood, and made a good hard run home, I and the two Boltonians I had met at Niarbyl Bay, and met again on the 'Lady of Man'. I had left Foxdale in the rain, I reached home still in the rain. Two brilliant central days, an indifferent first day and a thoroughly wet final day. Variety is the very spice of life!

In The
Highest Pennine.

High Cup Nick.

September 1932

Jo's enthusiasm runs high on the unexplored. When she is prospecting the possibilities of forgotten passes and ancient pathways she could not be happier, unless it be upon the actual exploration. Every dotted line across the hill-shading of our maps is sure to receive attention sooner or later. The fascination of the 'dotted line' dates from the first time she cast eyes on an Ordnance Survey in her earliest cycling days. Someone had informed her that all dotted lines are tracks, and Jo implicitly believing, set her heart upon a certain wavering, heavily emphasised line that passed from peak to peak in the rough regions of Shap, regardless of the laws of natural contour. The route lacked any track, but Jo's boundless enthusiasm carried her over a long series of disheartening obstacles before she discovered that she had been attempting to trace a county boundary!

In the course of time one learns to understand maps more thoroughly. Experience is a hard teacher, and in the case of exploring alleged tracks encumbered with a bicycle the lessons are sure to be remembered. Difficulties crop up which people who never leave the roads cannot imagine. It is generally believed that Britain is a settled country where Nature is well tamed, but that is far from the truth. A man may yet get lost and never be seen again, or may wander for days in desolate land without habitation of any sort. Paths over the mountains are often too faint to be traced with certainty; climatic conditions may be such as to make a moderately difficult passage impossible, even in summer. The person who frequents the solitudes faces, at times, pitiless conditions which call for determination and much careful thought. That is half the pleasure of it. He alone has the right to say if it is worthwhile.

High Cup Nick is a natural phenomena in the limestone of Cross Fell, and is reached by a track of sorts[7] between Teesdale and the Vale of Eden. The name, High Cup Nick, is very expressive. It fascinates. Jo had talked of it for months, a prelude to certain action at the first opportunity, for High Cup Nick is just beyond the range of an ordinary weekend. The chance came when the Cotton strike of 1932 took place. Jo works in the mill, I was unemployed. As it was desirable to cover much ground by Saturday evening, we arranged that Jo should leave Preston soon after noon, and I should follow with all speed from Bolton. By thus minimising delay we hoped to make camp on the high ground between Brough and Middleton-in-Teesdale, a hundred miles from home.

After a long dry spell, the weather had broken. A night or two of heavy rain and drenching showers during the day with strong westerly winds told too plainly of the best we could hope for. I started late, riding hard across the paths of many a fierce downpour until the turn for Quernmore valley put the wind dead behind. After tea I entered Lunesdale. The river was a swirl of spate; at Caton by Lancaster it flowed brown and full-lipped, encroaching the low fields; at Kirkby Lonsdale 12 miles higher the river boiled over the rocks in mad endeavour. All the twenty six miles of the Dale to Sedbergh were changing panoramas of threatening clouds in a windy sky, brown fells reflecting the sky in moods from sullen to gay, and always chattering waters within sound. Dusk in Rawtheydale, a gradually rising road, the noisy stream at hand, shapely mountains between which the road pursued a winding way. Cautley Spout was a white flake in a ravine already filled with night. Jo was still ahead; I lit my lamp and rode harder along the lonely highway, over its final steeper pitches to the black, windy summit from which the dim lights of Kirkby Stephen lay scattered below. At 9.30pm. in that highland railway town the silence of sleep had already settled. Under an inky canopy I crossed the Vale of Eden to Brough, that ancient, stone-built village clustered below the ruins of its castle. Brough lives in less fearful days now – Brough was abed and secure, with only the wind wandering abroad.

Jo was riding well. I had seen nothing of her, and felt the cold hand of doubt. Was she really ahead? I could only go on. The wild road that crawls over the fells to Middleton-in-Teesdale pulled me up, and I faced a long walk uphill. High above me a light flashed, and hopefully I signalled back.

---

7   Now part of the Pennine Way.

The light remained stationary, so I hurried until I came within hail. "Thank Heaven it is you!", came the response, "I'm tired out".

Jo had waited until after the usual time, then fearing I had got away early, she had hurried. For eighty miles we had chased each other with no more than a few minutes between us! Below the summit there was a bridge over a peaty burn; gratefully we camped in the lee of it.

The morrow began cold and stormy. A passing shepherd peeped in to congratulate us on the choice of a comfortable place on the rain-sodden fells and held our attention with tales of winter storms and inky mists when even these weathered old hill-men had lost themselves for hours at once.

Our journey eastwards crossed a high ridge at 1,574 feet and took us over miles of purple moorlands swept in turn by sun and rain, till Teesdale lay below, and we swooped down into Middleton. The main road up the dale gave us a hard struggle in the teeth of the wind. We saw the distant fleck and heard the roar of High Force a quarter of a mile away heading the steep ravine. The next half hour yielded three miles of hard pedalling to Langdon Beck, where we abandoned the highway. This road, on its way to Alston, becomes the highest main road in England at 1,942 feet. This is a land of high roads threading their difficult ways over the highest Pennine – the bleakest country below the Cheviot.

High Force.

Fig. 34: High Force

Behind a wall we shivered through lunch, a meal which terminated abruptly in a rush of rain. We tramped along a stony track for four desolate miles of successive summits, wind and rain raking us all the time, and ahead on Cross Fell, such a grey swirl of cloud as might dishearten less enthusiastic travellers. The track, in a shocking condition, tumbled us down to Cauldron Snout, that waterfall with the expressive name which must surely bring many people enquiring "what's in a name?" Normally the Tees descends a series of great steps; this day it was a raging slide of white water, fearful to look upon, and shaking the very earth about it. At the foot of Cauldron Snout, Maize Beck pours in, forming the angles of three counties, Durham, Cumberland and the North Riding of Yorkshire. A decrepit hut close by saved us from a terrific storm that swept down from Cross Fell with an awful show of cloud. By a small bridge above the falls we gained access to Cumberland, and following the course of Maize Beck, through several fields – hardly won intake from the predominant moors – crossed stiles and gates to Birkdale, reputed the loneliest farm in England. We had tea there.

No modern complications disturb life at Birkdale. The nearest neighbour lives two miles away, the nearest village is eight, and the nearest railway station eleven and a half. From the first of May until the end of September the postman comes twice a week (if necessary), but for the remaining seven months not at all, the reason for which is plain to see when one looks round at the vast wilderness of black fells and their intersecting maze of peat hags with brown becks, so often unfordable. The old farmer spoke of long weeks of isolation when the snow makes the whole region inaccessible, the search for buried sheep, the relief when all are safely penned and the stock warmly stabled. All life marks time, waiting patiently for the release of Spring. Four people and a tiny baby, then only ten weeks old, shut away from the outer world, provisioned already against the Autumn floods. The young woman with the baby turned to Jo and said with deep fervour, "Oh, if I could only go to the warm south for a few weeks!" Even then, so early in September, the great shoulders of the Pennine had the stamp of winter upon them. She feared the winter with her baby in mind, but the old farmer thought more of the big thaws that change the clean, far-stretching snow into wild torrents of water.

Our host displayed interest when we announced our intention to cross the fells to Dufton in Edendale, eight miles away. Came questions. Were we used to fell country? Did we know of the hundred traps set by nature and the weather-demon? They were manifold on Cross Fell. Unwary travellers are better away, initiating themselves on the more gentle hills of the south, not causing trouble and inconvenience to the shepherd folks at the busiest season. His tone softened at our reply. We were no plains-people out on a day trip. Not strangers to the hills. Our whole beings were wrapped up in them. They were our life, and our experience was nothing light or shadowy.

The discouragement was not unjust. People often come to Birkdale for the purpose of crossing High Cup Head, usually day-trippers woefully unprepared in the matter of clothing and equipment, expecting to find a kind of mild moorland footpath. As a rule they come back hours later, baffled. One party set off at noon in high summer, wandered through the day and night, and regained Birkdale by a mere chance at 4 am., utterly worn out. There was recalled the rare pluck of a girl who had twisted off the heels of both shoes, had limped through the night with a large nail drilling her foot, whilst both feet were badly cut and bleeding. She had suffered agonies, but had the spirit to smile and cheer the rest of the party. Commonly people came back to Birkdale later than midnight, begging for accommodation. The shepherd vigorously denied the existence of any track for the first two and a half miles, though the Ordnance Survey show one. He said he was willing to post the whole route if approached on the matter by the authorities, an offer that must be regarded as very generous. If there is mist about he advised nobody to cross.

The farmer led us to a position of vantage, the better to give us directions which, delivered in broad Lowland Scots, were difficult to understand. However, we had two excellent allies, a wind due west which we must keep to our faces, and clear weather in spite of the stormy skies.

The first cairn called Moss Shop was in full view. We gained it easily, afterwards bearing right on rising ground to cut out the great loop of Maize Beck, which we would have to cross later. By this means we also avoided the deeper peat hags or runnels, which are a problem to cross, often many feet deep with sheer yielding sides and water in them. They are a trap, sometimes almost impossible to get out of. The going was better than we had expected, rather wet and heavy, and slow with the loaded bikes. In truth our luck was in, for the hills were sharp and clear in spite of great banks of black cloud sailing like stately galleons, too high to be effective. In half an hour we passed between two small cairns our guide had called 'herricks', and farther along another cairn surrounded by thistles confirmed our direction. Now Maize Beck appeared, bearing across our line of vision from its headwaters on Rasp Hill.

Gazing round, we realised the force behind the Birkdale shepherd's warning. This is not a land for the street lover. Vast waves of brown and black moorland rose to black shoulders with black peaks beyond, the very heart of Cross Fell, the highest Pennine (2,902 feet), the wildest moorland in England. Not a tree nor a building, nor the track of man or beast lay within sight. The silence of it, the weird broodiness lay like a hand on us, for here we saw the primeval world, unchanging through the ages. It was all so magnificent; it entered into our innermost selves as we stared at the three-thousand feet altitudes so utterly desolate and forsaken.

Cross Fell is feared in the North country. It is the cradling place of the Helm Wind, that terrible local tornado so utterly foreign to these islands. This gale begins in a kind of southeasterly whirlwind and devastates everything in its path, throwing huge boulders into the air and even lifting the roofs off buildings made to withstand the the fierce winter gales of the district. Coming with the roar of an express train, it gives anyone caught in its trail a poor change indeed. Happily, the Helm Wind is a rare occurrence, and is entirely local and short-lived. The fell itself covers a great area of entirely trackless moorland, largely bog which is in many places capable of swallowing a man without leaving any traces of his existence. Nicholas Size, the Lakeland author, makes use of the Helm Wind in his book "The Secret Valley". He says:

"The phenomenon of the Helm Wind, which <u>sometimes lasts for three days</u>, is caused by a collision of two weather systems among the mountains. It generally originates in the long valley running North and South near Cross Fell, and it is said that the clouds coming up from the East do not mingle with those coming from the West, but form long lines with a lane of clear sky between them; and the wind beneath forms an acute disturbance over a curiously localised area, which is sometimes in one valley, sometimes in another."

I underline the 'sometime lasts for three days' because other authorities on this phenomenon do not agree with this. Maize Beck was our guide. Gradually we descended to it, traversed the bank for a likely crossing. The fording was knee-deep, icy cold, and not very comfortable to bare feet. Fortune again favoured us; we had no difficulty in finding a promised cairn from where a soft turfy track the width of a main road led us up the brown slope – the 'green band' of the Birkdale Prophet. With a last sharp climb we were in the Pass, rejoicing that without a falter we had crossed a corner of the dreaded wastes of Cross Fell.

With breathless suddenness, in the middle of the Pass, we came upon High Cup Nick. This is a tremendous ravine, 500 feet deep, scooped from the solid bed of the pass in some unremembered convulsion, some ice-age never known. The two sides, viewed from the head, are as identical as if they had been neatly clipped by some unimaginable scoop wielded by some impossible hand. One might call it a monstrous cup laid on its side, so the name of it is extremely apt. Far beyond, framed in the inverted arc of High Cup Nick, lay the Vale of Eden, rumpled and very green. Our track was now distinct, an arduous scramble along the northern lip, suggesting danger in misty weather. At the highest point we topped 2,000 feet.

Dusk came; we were ready to camp, but where water ran the chaotic rocks prohibited a pitch, and where green turf sprang beautifully underfoot water was entirely absent. The darkening Vale lay in a huge sweep far below; towards Lakeland the mountains were already gathering the indistinctness of nightfall about them, and the foothills ahead of us rose in shapely billows of barren greenery. Now encountering rock and loose scree, now on tangly heather, we hurried down to a gate, through a sheep pen, and reached a track we could ride, down, down, into the fold of the foothills a thousand feet below, where we found water and the most comfortable campsite. Supper was a lazy period of supreme content, when Jo, at least, was happy in the retrospect of another conquest. Came the steady drumming of the rain, and with it the muffled blackness of the Styx fell upon the fells.

The morning was clear and breezy. Two full days ahead of us amongst the tempting scenery of the Dales; behind us – towering above us, in fact, Cross Fell and High Cup Nick. There was desire for hurry.

Fig. 35: The Old Mill, Hawes

Appleby is a venerable little town, very quiet, very clean, and the river Eden which flows serenely through the heart of the town is also very clean. Its lovely situation in the middle of the valley has no doubt been many times cursed by its citizens of the Middle Ages when, constantly harassed by the fierce Border raiders, it was often sacked and burned, and the people massacred. There are relics of those very uncertain days in the fine old church which dates its first rector from the year 1070. And on the tablets lining the walls one may read names familiar in the bloody pages of English history.

From Appleby to Kirkby Stephen are ten miles of crinkly lanes and old world village drenched with the turbulent history of the North. A happier relic is the village maypole at Warcop, still, I believe, the centre of the May Day festivities. A gossiping woman at a restaurant in Kirkby Stephen kept us until dirty weather came rolling down the Dales. Up the long depression of Mallerstang we were at times beaten to a standstill by wind and rain until the turn to Hawes at the Moorcock junction gave us the favour of Boreas, down to Hardraw.

At the head of a ravine which is effectively barred by the property of the Green Man Inn is the famous Hardraw Force. A notice board invites people to view the fall and 'enquire at the hotel'. As much from principle as from motives of economy, we opened the gate, passed through some henpens, and, quite aware that we were being watched, we boldly (or brazenly) walked to the fall. In full spate, it presented a magnificent picture, pouring over a lip and falling eighty feet sheer onto an islet of rock which smashed the smooth glass of it into a million flying spraylets. A path passing behind the Force enabled us to look through the wall of water, ourselves guarded from the remotest splash. This peculiarity is shared to some degree by Thornton Force near Ingleton. The once beautiful vicinity is ruined by a bandstand, an artificial shrubbery, and some refreshment huts, empty and rotting in the damp atmosphere. I shudder to think of it during the height of a holiday weekend. As we walked back a man locked the gate, approached us, and quietly diverted us to the hotel. Still bold (or brazen) we walked through the building, out at a side door, and were well awheel before the astonished innkeeper could challenge us.

Wensleydale was lovely in a light drizzle like a half revealing veil, heightened by evening tranquillity as we passed down the east side on a road that lifted and fell as gently as a breath. From old Askrigg we crossed the swollen Ure by a wooden bridge to Aysgarth, then a quiet lane into Bishopdale, a minor Dale that always seems to impart a rich atmosphere of settled prosperity (a rare thing to capture in these days).

Still raining, dusk creeping down, and a hard face-wind, the road gradually ascending by the river. Jo remembered a sheltered nook above Cray Gill, but that is overlooking

Fig. 36: Hardraw Force

KETTLEWELL

Fig. 37: Kettlewell

Wharfedale and we had little stomach to struggle another thousand feet, wet and hungry. The hedged roadside offered no camping spaces.

Bishopdale narrowed; the misty fells closed and loomed ahead; the road tilted, bringing us from the saddle. Where we might have snatched a campsite the wind, now awake again, howled defiance. The summit of Kidstones Pass, grey, cold, unreal in a shifting half-night. We began to descend; a swing left, a swing right, a straight drop, till, where a small aspiring Hardraw Force breasted a diminutive cliff we pulled up, and behind a wall we found all the space and shelter we wanted. A sanctuary there, where was cooked the simplest of orchard fare, and superlative smells floated out of a dry tent door to mingle with the rain-mists wandering on Kidstones Fell.

Now the last, easy day, with home a bare fifty miles away. At breakfast we had the roar of the little Hardraw for accompaniment. A hundred yards away a copious streamlet showed in half a dozen gleaming places half a dozen white cascades. A mist cut the fell tops into ridges of perfect evenness; Wharfedale, below, was faintly green through the everlasting drizzle.

There was no hurry. We kept as close as may be to the brimming

Fig. 38: A View of the Bridge

Fig. 39: Rest and be Thankful

Wharfe, on the road that hugs the east bank from Kettlewell. At Kilnsey, across the river, great activity prevailed, for this was Showday, and Kilnsey Show, any Dalesman will tell you, brings forth magnificent stock. Wharfedale is always very beautiful, easily reached, but no less pleasant for that, and at monolith-crowned Rylstone, where we branched west for Ribblesdale, the bonnie heather gleamed a warm purple. The crinkly plain by Gargrave, the unsteady lanes of the Pendle country, and with Pendle itself looming high in the borrowed grandeur of mists, and final familiar roads homewards – always a reluctant way.

While plotting another 'dotted line' route, Jo keeps an eye on High Cup Nick, and the further possibilities of the Highest Pennine.

Peckforten and Beeston Castles.

THE SECRET CAMPING SITE.   June 4. 1932.

Fig. 40: Peckforten and Beeston Castles

Flaming June merited its title but little on the patch of sward amid the pines of Peckforton Hills where Jo and I passed a night. But the sun the next morning! Warm beams slanting through the trees were upon us by eight-o-clock, making the rising a more genial business than the retiring had been. Where we consorted the troublesome north-easter passed harmlessly overhead, and the hot sunshine poured down untempered.

It is great fun dodging gamekeepers. In the ten or twelve counties within our weekend range we have camped regularly on the best preserves of the 'landed gentry', a thrilling sport as a rule with, at the worst, only the prospect of having to make a hurried nocturnal flitting. This we have so far managed to avoid. This particular Saturday night, as we padded a silent path just within the shelter of a pine wood, we made the disconcerting discovery that we were being watched by three pairs of eyes. An open pasture lay along the edge of the wood, and across it three men stood, following our movements closely whenever they could see us. We must have been vague at the distance, and as we were behind a low wall we guessed our bicycles to be invisible. Remembering a cave near at hand we dumped the machines there, and to throw the watchers off the scent, we continued to walk, following the path round the edge of the field in their direction. The ruse succeeding, they let us pass with no more than a joke. They were obviously gamekeepers, and saw, in us, nothing more remarkable than a pair of lovers strolling on the hills.

Having thus disposed of their suspicions, we took a circuitous route through the depth of the forest to our bikes again, got our water bucket, and set off through the glade for Harthill in quest of water. As the bicycles were safely hidden in the furthest depth of the cave, we were easy enough in mind and went singing loudly along. In such a country as mid-Cheshire where the hills are too low to produce any sizeable surface stream, the water difficulty is acute. Without it the most wonderful campsite in the world soon becomes mean. Our search was successful in about a mile; we were half-way along the return path when approaching voices startled us, and we had no time but to drop the bucket in the young bracken before the three keepers sauntered into view. These men, still unsuspecting of the true reason for our presence, bantered us for a few minutes, the while we played up to them, desperately striving to keep their attention from straying towards the canvas bucket, which seemed to stick up and proclaim its presence. We knew well that once their suspicions were awakened it would be hopeless to try and camp anywhere near these hills, as they must know every nook and hollow – and their orders were absolute.

At last, with a parting humour they passed on, and we breathed freely again, scarcely believing their trained eyes had entirely overlooked the telltale bucket, to our guilty eyes the most conspicuous thing on the Peckforton Hills. This time we tracked the keepers until they properly disappeared, heading for Harthill, and doubtless, the congenial atmosphere of the local tavern. Then, quite comfortable at last, we toiled up to the hilltop cave, and the secret camp site set so deeply in the heart of the woods that we defy anyone to sight it from any path.

From the isolated 350 ft. rock on which are the 13th century ruins of Beeston Castle, the Peckforton Hills stretch southwards for about eight miles. Near the northern end stands the modern castle of Peckforton, built in the Norman style, its many sandstone towers rising above the trees. Most of the range is densely wooded, and, under the Marquis of Cholmondeley, is well ranged by watchful keepers.

June 1932

OUR BERWYN CROSSINGS.

"Old farms with mossed-stone fences, old grassy roads that wind
For ever on and upward to higher fields behind;
By ancient bush-grown pastures bestrewn with boulders grey,
And lonely meadow-slopes that bear thin crops of upland hay.

As, terrace over terrace, we climb the mountain stair,
More solitary grow the ways, more wild the farms, and rare;
And slenderer in their rocky beds the singing brooks that go
Down skipping to the valley stream a thousand feet below"

Henry A. Beers[8]

Draw a line between Chirk and Bala Lake. There, for a direct distance of
rather more than twenty miles is bisected a long range of high moorlands
called the Berwyns. For thirty of its loveliest miles the River Dee flows at
Berwyn's feet. Until quite recently (about 1938) not a single road of quality
crossed the long chain, and even now (1940s) the one fair road, reconstruc-
ted, over Milltir Cerig (Stony Mile) is quite impassable for most of the
winter months. There are roads – of a sort. Three roads, steep, gated, high.
There is the westernmost, Bwlch-y-Groes (Pass of the Cross), perhaps not
quite Berwyn, but at least in the line of continuity. This, at 1,790 ft., claims
to be the highest 'carriage' road in Wales, and on both sides crosses the face

---

8   For those of you who enjoy the wilder parts of Wales, this is Charlie Chadwick's 'trailer' for one such
     story which follows and could be kept in mind for other stories of his.

Fig. 41: Bwlch-y-Groes on the Bala-Dinas Mawddwy road

of a sheer precipice. Its surface is atrocious. Then comes Bwlch Rhiw Hirnant, at 1,641 ft., from Bala to Lake Vyrnwy, all gates, ruts, and boulders. The Milltir Cerig, at 1,638 ft., is the third, the only practicable road for traffic. Allt-y-Bady may be called a road between Llangollen and Glyn Ceiriog; it is only 1,279 ft. high, and it is only three miles long, but the gradient on each side is fierce. This part of Berwyn, between Llangollen and Chirk is really an eastern spur, or ridge, little more than half the general altitude of the main range.

These roads are lovely and wild, with always fine views. To cyclists they are well known, and we have frequently used them all in our passage from north to south or vice versa. But what of the tracks, those four or five paths which make their way through the bog, the bracken, over dizzy heights? Amongst cyclists the Berwyn tracks are classics. Many adventurous wheelmen during the last two decades have manhandled their machines over these grim mountains, and their stories have been told wherever wheelmen foregather. They are not strange, even to our inquisitive wheels, and they have led us into some tight corners, into some real feats of endurance. The would-be 'pass-stormer' will find the Berwyns a very accommodating range. They will give him a simple start in his arduous calling. Roads like Hirnant Pass will give him 'lick'. Probably Nant Rhyd Wilym

Fig. 42: Llangollen

will follow, a fine route, and quite easy, of moderate altitude (1,591 ft.). Then Plas Nantyr, to try out his map reading capabilities, his ability to cross swamps, his patience. Then, perhaps, he will graduate; the fever will (or will not!) be in his blood, and the finest things in Berwyn will fall to him, the difficult Maen Gwynedd (2,288 ft.) and the really hectic Moel Sych track 2,600 ft. but a few feet from the highest summit. The dry, long days of summer will be chosen first, and when thinking on it sometime later he may try them in the winter.

We have crossed some of these Berwyn tracks in the depths of the winter. They are not hectic experiences – they are desperate adventures with even tragic possibilities 'in the bag'. I have in mind a late autumn ride from Lancashire, with Moel Sych sandwiched between, 172 miles in a single day. They were mad times, those. Jo and I are still mad, as the reader may now judge…….

Fig. 43: Hirnant Pass

November 24/25 1934

The four of us gathered for tea in Chester, Fred and Bob with single bicycles, and Jo (his wife-to-be) and I with the tandem. November twilight had transformed the city into a lamplit pleasance, the deeper shadows hiding jarring modernity's in the medieval structure. We had, however, little time to wander about old Chester, with Cynwyd Youth Hostel over thirty miles across the border hills. Hostel wardens frown on late arrivals.

The miles fly when a sturdy wind pushes dead behind, and the road is clear of traffic. A black night – one could almost feel the low clouds overhead, but the windings and branchings of the first border miles are familiar stuff, and the preliminary heavings of the plain were taken in good style. The hills closed – felt rather than seen – we climbed the glen from Tryddyn, full of the music of a running stream, industrial scars hidden by the kindly night, and finally topped the open moor to Llandegla. The fast road to Corwen, leaping, curving, falling; a lively tandem that could hardly be kept in check; the straining eyes in the darkness, the catching of familiar objects as they flew past like phantasms; the nice judging of this sudden bend, that remembered swoop, and finally the jumble of lights appearing in the opening valley to tell us of Corwen and the Holyhead road.

At the Old Mill at Cynwyd we busied ourselves with supper preparations. The Hostel was rapidly filling as, wary of hostel ways, we claimed our blankets and seized our hammocks by right of possession. Nobody baulked at an early 'lights out'. The sleepiness of winter was in the eyes of morning, in the naked beauty of the nodding trees edging the stream which

Fig. 44: King Charles' Tower, Chester

tumbles by the Old Mill, on its way to the parent Dee below. The clouds plodded steadily on their south-easterly course without a hint of sun, but set fair against rain. With the rough chances of fortune we might have, at least, a dry day for our Berwyn crossing. Our old miller-warden was not enthusiastic about the path below Cerig Coediog. Quite probably we would miss the track in the tangles below the pass, and even should we gain the summit the path beyond was of the imagination. We ought to have believed him, but we put our faith in Saint Bartholomew.

A rough land climbed above the stream, with beautiful glimpses of the ravine. We talked awhile with two local early birds whose particular worm was a two gallon can of fine whinberries. They advised us not to go to Cynwyd Falls. The last time I had seen the falls was at Easter 1926 with the 'We.R.7' (a select group of hardriders) and they were a lovely spectacle, set in a rocky niche below the hills. Now the vandal electricity has claimed the water, and only in the stormiest weather does a vestige of their former grace return. We plodded on, snatching an occasional ride, into the great cup-like hollow below Moel Ferna. Here the Trystion stream wandered, gathering strength from a dozen aimless rivulets. A dog barked at the last lonely farm; an afforestation of fir trees marked the end of the road. Thereafter a track.

In the centre of the 'basin', glowing with a tangle of bracken and ling, our map bade us cross the diminutive Trystion. Immediately afterwards the path completely vanished. There was a shallow gap of a pass away to the east, but our route was obviously aslant Cerig Coediog, and we laboured up the slope, sneaking higher on tufted moor-grass. With the tandem it was hard work, even with Jo straining behind, but soon we came to an impasse of heather. Fred and Bob shouldered their bikes and crashed on; the tandem was not so tractable. The kit was taken off, all surplus weight passed into Jo's keeping, and I forced the tandem across my shoulders. The scramble that followed remained painfully vivid for a long time afterwards. The heather was a dense, tough growth almost waist deep; underneath the ground was all rocks, loose stones, little channels, small hummocks. The general angle was at least 45 degrees. I stumbled over ground I could only feel; the rocks constantly caught at my feet, the whip like branches held me, catapulted me forward, tore at my clothing, my knees, the dipped front wheel, which was plucked down with further disaster to my aching shoulders. Sometimes I flopped down involuntarily, sometimes I stopped to regain wind and strength for the next pitch. And Jo gamely struggled ahead to choose the clearest way, to warn me, to guide, both arms full of cycle bags. Fred and Bob topped the ridge with no voice left for triumph. I arrived a bad fourth, feeling as if I had been a ball in a rugby scrum, and quite exhausted. Our altitude was about 2,000 ft. The wind blew cold on our perspiring bodies, and there was a sardonic note in it. We looked over the ridge and stared into a great, desolate hollow. Below us were beetling crags. So the great battle up the hill had been in vain. In the best grace possible we dipped into that eastward pass, frittering away three hundred feet of sheer hard labour. Then we picked up the track! Now it was better, on the open moor. Our track was one great rut. When the bed of the hollow was reached, it vanished completely again, and we were in the middle of a stagnant swamp. Now the difficulties of oozy slime and a slimy stream with

Fig. 45: Down into the Glyn Valley

quivering banks. To escape it we heaved bikes and tandem over a wall, and a few minutes later we gladly heaved them back again to escape worse. We hailed a rushing stream with delight, but were soon disillusioned as we were forced back again into the shaking bog. One suggested making for higher ground; we splashed across wearily, and, quite suddenly, walked on to our will o' wisp track, its one great rut never more welcomed.

At a marked improvement in the way stood a spacious hut, open-fronted. There we recuperated, brewed gallons of hot tea on our Primus stoves, tried to dry our chilled feet ere replacing soaked footwear, and recounted to each other the tribulations attending cyclist pass-stormers. Five hours had passed on our crossing of Cerig Coediog, and eighty miles lay ahead of us still. Riding became possible. We dipped down a magnificent little ravine into the beautiful estate of Plas Nantyr. A hilly lane carried us on the edge of the moor until we overlooked the placid Glyn Valley, already withdrawing into the dusk of a short winter day. A dozen hairpin bends dropped us into Glyn Valley and then the fast road by Glyn Ceiriog to Chirk seemed heavenly after our rough way across the Berwyns.

In Wrexham darkness had come. We bade good-day to Fred, who was for tea in Chester again, and his direct route home. Our way was over the rumply Marches, under the castled pile of Caergurle, and to the Dee at Queensferry. We dawdled not at tea there, in a room as cold as the shooting hut, but made for the warm saloon of the Rock Ferry boat. From Liverpool our pedals beat steady rhythm – rhythm that gradually faltered until, on the

Fig. 46: Lathkil Dale

last mile, three pairs of legs admitted their weakness, and only just carried their owners upstairs to bed at midnight.

Fig. 47: Over Moel Sych

September, 1932, like 'the Lady April' had her full share of moods. One associates this lovely month with bountiful harvest, with sunshine and blue skies, a period of settled weather through which creeps approaching autumn. But this month was tearful, sunny, shaken by gales, frost and calm and hot, mixing all the varieties of our English climate into an April pot-pourri.

On the third Saturday afternoon I crossed Chat Moss under the bluest of skies. Little puffs of white cloud floated slowly along, and the sun was hot, like full summer. I moved quickly, as one who has many miles to cover in few hours, for Jo and Fred would be awaiting me ninety miles away, and they had promised to have a grand supper awaiting my arrival. Although adding a few miles I took the Tarporley road in preference to the main road by Chester and Chirk. I was on roads that make hurry possible. The little hills and long levels of this familiar highway, with a light breeze behind, kept my feet circling quickly; unconsciously, as my mind travelled with my eyes along the hedges and into cottage gardens. Twelve years before I had first timidly crept along here in a mood of discovery, my wondering senses in a growing delight of new sights and scenes, and now I appreciated it just as much, looking forward to the next bend just as keenly, though I had turned that bend a hundred times. There is something great about the way one can travel the same old roads so many times in the same spirit of enthusiasm. It would break one's heart to know that never again could one's face be set towards them. Death were better!

I appreciate suitable company, but when an alien voice breaks upon a mental ecstasy, I curse silently, and answer with an eloquent semi-silence. This voice announced a desire to be listened to for the next ten miles to Bunbury – ten of the loveliest, most expectant, miles. At least he had a turn of speed, so we whipped along until the lane which led him to his lady-love appeared, and I found myself alone again. Eleven miles to Whitchurch, easy, glorious miles, with the red hills of Peckforton to the west, a roaming place on many a Sunday with Tom in the past nine years. Two miles from Whitchurch, on the Shropshire border a tandem pair caught up to me, and boasted how they had come all the way from Burtonwood by St Helens. I agreed they had done a good ride (almost as far as I had) but when they complained of the hard road I laughed. "You'll have harder yet!" I forecasted, as, entering Whitchurch, I sent them on to the Wellington road, myself turning westward in an oblique slant towards the Welsh border.

A few miles along the Ellesmere road I stopped for tea at a cottage all but hidden in a long riot of a garden. Fifty six miles were good enough for an afternoon ride. Now the level waters of the Mere, the narrow streets of Ellesmere, the crossing of the Holyhead road at Whittington, where the great towers and moat of a feudal castle add romance to the place. I have heard it said that here was born the poor boy who dreamed of London streets paved with gold, and who became the Capital's greatest Lord Mayor three times. Behind the fairy story of Dick Whittington is the germ of truth. Saturday night in Oswestry, narrow streets, great crowds, dusk – and the road again, beating south again as the moon came up. There is a cross roads at Llynclys, and there I turned westwards, between low hills, growing higher, with a river growing swifter, clearer, the Tanat river. Lamplit, in moonlight, a road almost level, are ideal conditions of travel, and my wheels sped for many miles, veered at last from the main valley, and came to Llanrhaeadr-yn-Mochnant, the deep village under the shadow of Berwyn. The last four miles above the Rhaeadr stream would shatter any dream of speed, the ninety miles in my legs began to tell their tale, and my mind was occupied with the promised supper, now so near. I had earned it, I felt. After an array of good things there was to be plum pudding overspread with custard. Two helpings. Then I would lie back in supreme comfort when it was over, and smoke a reminiscent cigarette.

There was Pistyll Rhaeadr ahead, a tall black cliff shutting up the valley, with the white streak of water upon it, a farm, even a group of great fir trees dwarfed by this, the highest waterfall in Wales. On the last hill above the farm I turned aside through a gate, along a good green track, and at the first bend I saw our two tents romantically placed across the track – the only level spot in that region. The tents were unlit and deserted; inside I saw the rest of the kit hurriedly thrown down. Leaned against the steep moor were the two bicycles. Then I saw the table. This was a huge, flat-topped rock about two feet high. For lack of other space Fred had encircled it within the tent, one large section protruding from the doorway. And even the table was bare!

My light had evidently been seen, for there were voices calling me from somewhere far below in the bottom of the valley. Some time later two over-heated cyclists burst through the bracken below the path, carrying a milk-can and a canvas bucket. They had foraged the farm without luck, and tak-ing a short cut along this branch valley had become tangled up in fences, heather, and bog.

Long afterwards the pudding appeared, if not hot and steaming, at least warm on the outside. Of custard there was none, but we sat round our rocky table in the bright moonlight and ate, and drank coffee ad lib, and yarned. The 'table' effectively stopped us from closing up the tent, so Fred and I slept curled round it.

Cool and sulky morning. How often has serene eventide lulled our last thoughts into a golden morrow, to find, on awakening, a transformation, a promise falsified. The rain barely held off while we packed our kit away, and as we moved on in single file along the narrowing path the rain came, "gentle as the dew from heaven" at first, then steadily settling in, in true Berwyn fashion. At a stream the track ended, the trouble began, the usual becaped struggle over tufty grass, tangly heather, into the wild amphitheatre in which lie reed-edged, gloomy Llyn Llyncaws, under the frowning brow of Moel Sych. As this was our third crossing we feared no false moves, and skirted the lake, striking by the easiest route, towards a rugged summit ridge directly north. There is no easy way, with heavily laden bicycles that first summit was reached by sheer hard graft. The cumbrous capes, the slip-ping grass, brought us down in turns, and we fell heavily. The heather tugged at us. This ridge gave a view into the deep jaws of Maen Gwynedd valley, across which the rain slanted. Now the climb was toward Moel Sych itself, aslant the main spur, again a devilish struggle, this time with loose scree to cross, over which one looked down hundreds of feet of rock to Llyn Llyncaws. I was well ahead when I saw Jo suddenly slip and come down, bicycle and all on the very edge of the cliff. Fred dropped his bike and made a grab, hauling her clear, with not a foot of space nor a moment of time to spare. Dangerous moments! No injuries, just a word of thanks, and once more the slow, wary plod with shouldered bikes. These things are not remarkable, just the rough chances of the hills which the three of us are willing to take.

A tiny 'gateway' of a gap in the rock heralded the summit, and hot and winded we threw ourselves down. Our altitude was 2,600 ft.; the great backbone of Berwyn heaved away with its many ribs eastward. Llyn Llyn-caws lay a thousand feet below in dark reflection, a pear shaped mirror. On the northern side, miles of bog-ridden moorland slopes wasting away into the rain. Nothing more, except the sense of vastness and a great solitude.

Now the long descent, three miles and more of wary treading. Again we were fortified by past experience. The exultation of winning to a difficult summit is apt to vanish when the subsequent descent becomes so involved that one wearies of even hoping to get down to sane, hard roads again, and we shall never forget such an experience in rain and bog when every step had become a labour, every movement an effort, every vista a morale-shattering vista of endless acres of shaggy tussocks emphasised by boggy runnels that were more to be feared than the bitter tops. That is when one begins to long for the easy pleasure of just lying down and perhaps sleeping, sleeping on and on… for ever. We had learned the way, striking down the slope of Nant Esgeiriau, remaining sufficiently above the watercourses to avoid shouldering the heavy bikes again. The rain ceased – perhaps we got below the clouds – and at a farmhouse called Rhuol we reached the old road which runs up Cwm Pennant to join the Milltir Cerig. There we tried to make ourselves look less disreputable, changed into dry stockings (but kept on soaked shoes), started the Primus stoves, and did ourselves well on the rest of our food.

Fig. 48: Splashing through

Jo was the lucky one for once; she had a day or two to spare, and gathering together our kit, bade us au revoir, to penetrate deeper into Merioneth. Fred and I, with over eighty miles yet to cover, turned our wheels eastward from Llandrillo, through the Vale of Edeyrnion to Corwen, laboured over the Llande-gla Moors to a belated tea at Chester.

In the quiet glow of evening, with September once again in her golden mood, we planned our next hill-crossing, little dismayed by the hostile reception Moel Sych seems to hold against our persistent wooing.

By the way, Moel Sych means 'Dry Hill'.

The "West Arms" at Llanarmon. D.C.   Popular rendezvous of Berwyn 'Pass-Stormers'.

Fig. 49: The West Arms at Llanarmon, popular with Berwyn 'Pass-stormers'

Fig. 50: The Lwrch Valley

July 1941

"What subtle witchcraft man constrains
To change his pleasures into pains?"

Denham

Maen Gwynedd, as a 'rough stuff' Berwyn passage takes second place only to Moel Sych. Indeed, on certain points it is more difficult, as it is longer, if over 300 ft. lower, and the approaches for we northern cyclists are far more complicated. From Llanarmon, at the head of Glyn Valley there is the tough ascent of Cefn-yr-Odfa, to be followed by a rough track over a 1,600 ft. ridge down into the long Iwrch Valley, itself a long drag on a shambles of a road. The direct approach by the whole of the Iwrch makes a complicated and hilly loop some miles longer. Maen Gwynedd itself is, on the ascent to the summit, like Moel Sych, quite trackless, although a path of sorts is then picked up – to dip and climb yet another summit. Perhaps because of kindlier weather, I have found Maen Gwynedd the finer of the two in point of scenery and views.

My desire was to introduce Jo to Maen Gwynedd, and, incidentally, to make my third crossing; the previous ones being both with Fred way back in 1929 and 1930. Our plans were made. Jo would entrain to Liverpool in the early afternoon, and crossing the Wirral, would ride for Glyn Valley. I was to slip away from work in Manchester, ride hard across Cheshire, and we would meet in Glyn Valley, possibly at Llanarmon DC at 9 pm. Distant rendezvous – over 80 miles! Together we would find a camp-site about Cefn-yr-Odfa or the Iwrch Valley, and for that purpose we carried between us a skeleton kit, ruthlessly cutting out all non-essentials. We merely carried the lightest of tents without flysheet, a ground sheet, one eiderdown quilt, one Primus stove and two aluminium nesting pans. We were assured daylight until midnight[9], and hoped for good weather.

At noon I slipped off my overalls and started the long run across County Palatine. The sun was hot, there was no wind – a perfect day for cycling. Mere, some miles beyond Altrincham provided lunch. Then the Chester road, the easy, swinging Cheshire plain, through Northwich. Near Sandiway I turned into remembered lanes, a labyrinth of leafy beauty, free from traffic by Whitegate, Oulton Park, flowery Eaton down to Beeston Castle station, past the ancient ruins and along that lovely byway which hugs Peckforton Hills. I had tea at Malpas, almost on the further edge of the County, in a cool room, where the table belied the grim realism of war. Then down to Bangor-on-Dee, with time to spare. This was well spent swimming in a quiet reach of the river near Overton Bridge. There was a heavy drag up to Ruabon, where I joined Jo's route, and on that sweep down to the Dee again near Cefr, I saw her, far ahead.

ON THE
BEESTON - MALPAS ROAD.
NEAR
BICKERTON.

Fig. 51: On the Beeston-Malpas road near Bickerton

9   Wartime double summer time.

The meeting was well timed on the outskirts of Chirk, and we lounged awhile in a sweet garden over coffee and cakes. Glyn Valley was at its loveliest, and after the hard riding how pleasant it was to potter along beside the little Ceiriog stream all the eleven varied miles to Llanarmon DC. A short distance beyond Llanarmon, along a gated track just below the farm of Gyrchynan-isaf, with the formidable Cefn-hir-Fynydd rearing above us, we found a lovely spot beside a stream, and there pitched our tent in the afterglow of a warm sunset.

That, indeed, was lightweight cycle camping in perfection. Under ideal conditions we had wedged our way into a tiny remote valley, right under the huge bulk of Berwyn. A leisured supper, then the chuckling brook to lull us into a sound sleep – and on the early morrow to break gently into our waking senses. The promise was kept – a blue morning betokening great heat; a vigorous wash, breakfast, and the speed packing of our simple outfit. We had talked with a passing farmer in the slow dusk of the evening, and he had promised a direct path into the Iwrch Valley, saving the loop over Cefn-hir-Fynydd and Cefn-yr-Odfa.

Fig. 52: Near Oulton Park

Our sweet little valley soon came to a blind; the narrow road switched up to the farm of Pen-cae-newydd. And an old rut of a track continued in a great sweep above the ravine. Very quickly we became involved in deep bracken. There was no alternative but to fight our way through the stuff, as tall as ourselves. Sure enough we were becoming involved in a major 'stunt' as a prelude, and we spent over an hour forcing a problematical way along the mountainside of Rhos (2,030 ft.). Cefn-hir-Fynydd was, by comparison, simple! Eventually we broke through to good turf – and no path at all, but we had our bearing, and soon the grand remoteness of Iwrch Valley lay below us, its hills dappled under summer clouds. On the way down we passed several bomb-craters, newly made, and could only conjecture the spirit of fear which made the German raider jettison his cargo in such a place! We reached the Iwrch at a bridge at Tyn-y-rhos, at 11 am., almost three hours 'out', and not three miles covered.

Then came the shambles of a road, ascending an utterly deserted valley to its final head at the fragmentary ruins called Blaen-y-Cwm. In this great amphitheatre, headed by highest Berwyn peaks, 2,500 to 2,700 ft. high, the long abandoned quarries and workmen's houses scattered about intensified the desolation. I have heard of cyclists camping at Blaen-y-Cwm, and spending an uneasy night for no clear reason... and even lunch parties on hot days being disturbed by chilly little winds wandering about the ruins. There resides here a strange atmosphere one cannot define, as if generations of miner-quarry folks have left behind something more of themselves than an old road leading to gaunt ruins, in a wild recess of the hills. Our faces turned to the north, where, twelve hundred feet above, across two miles of trackless moor, the ridge of Maen Gwynedd lay clear to the sky, and after a preliminary skirmish with bicycles over tufty hummocks, we sat down to eat and boil our water on the stove, and look back across the ruins to an opposite ridge....the ridge for Moel Sych! How common it is for travellers bound for Moel Sych to cross the ridge and unwittingly wander down to Blaen-y-Cwm, with the option of toiling back again for a thousand feet, or going over Maen Gwynedd.

There was heavy climbing under a broiling sun, the old game of pushing, carrying, recalcitrant bicycles, sweeping slightly eastwards to avoid a wire fence and the boggy beginnings of the River Iwrch. At length we gained the post on Craig Berwyn, at 2,288 ft., and flung ourselves down on the warm turf, with the brown ridges of Berwyn, height beyond height trailing away towards the eastern plain.

To the west, far below, the green vale of Dee towards Bala, the fine Merionith peaks of Arenig, Moelwyn above Ffestiniog, the knife-like Aran

Mawddwy, and far away, in a blue mist of distance, the mere suggestion of Ultima Thule, Y Wyddfa.

We had a fair track now, a sweep down a great hollow, and up again under the brow of Brwdd Arthur, for Maen Gwynedd is a deceiver and has two summits with a disheartening gap between. All the way down there were unfolding views facing us, ample reward in itself for the toiling climb, and lower down we were able to ride in a madcap sort of way, on a turfy path wriggling through the heather. We 'drummed up' again by a sheep-pen, in love with the view, and the sweet Vale of Edeyrnion now only a short distance below us. The hour was getting late when we reached the good road (how good!) running to Cynwyd, but there was time to swim in the river by the ancient bridge. We rode hard from Corwen up to Llandegla Moors, and at Rhydtalog dined well at the hotel by way of celebration.

In the cool of the evening we crossed the Wirral to New Ferry, and reached Exchange Station just in time for Jo to catch her train at 9 pm. I might have succumbed to the railway too, but the line was still out of action by reason of the winter 'blitz', and the last Bolton train, starting from Kirkdale was already on its way. There was no time to waste, yet just time to reach home lampless, and it was no hardship to ride on such a night, even on such a road as lay through Prescot, St Helens and the Wigan coalfield. At Hindley I punctured. In a trice I was surrounded by squatting colliers full of advice. Water was forthcoming at a word when I had difficulty in locating the hole, then one, on hearing that I was lampless, slipped quietly away and returned with two electric lamps. That is typical of the miner! At precisely midnight there finished a weekend when Berwyn smiled his best, and the long brown trails were sheer delight.

OBSERVATIONS and REFLECTIONS.   Easter, 1934

WHEN Easter comes the highway hums
(Like it always hums when Easter comes)
The livelong day with a rare array
Of miscellaneous roadsters gay.
        All of them off on a holiday!

Brief liberty—a world set free—
A moving scene of pageantry:
The land is gay in Spring array.
From town and city bent on play,
        The world is making holiday!

There's a tandem old with it's riders bold,
(What tales that tandem could unfold!)
And the riders gray, whose youthful day
Is like their tandem's, years away.
        Both of them off on a holiday!

And the youngsters green, perhaps over-keen,
Each of them perched on an aged machine,
As forth they sway in a wayward way
From peep o'dawn till the end of day.
        All of them off on a holiday!

Oh, what delight from morn till night,
Be Easter dull or be it bright.
And what care they for another day—
Today will soon be yesterday—
Today they are all on holiday!

Fig. 53: Observations and Reflections

Fig. 54: Ullswater to Glenridding

At Sadgill Farm we abandoned our normal modes of travel, three bicycles, a motorcycle and pillion, and from saddlebags and panniers tipped
out all the varied items of camping kit, to be replaced in five modest rucksacks. As receptacles the former were much more generous, so that what to
take and what to reject became a problem as knotty as how best to fill those
which must be carried across our backs. We began by rejecting the strictly
unnecessary, then packed first those things to be turned out last, and little
by little filled each bag to ten degrees of comfort and ninety degrees of ca-
pacity. As a large proportion of our equipment was food for four days, we
looked forward to starting each morning with substantially less to carry. If
the load was great at first, it would not again be so much, we argued, and
set out willing packmen, in a great show of holiday spirits.

We were five, Tom and Lucy – who rode up on Tom's motorcycle pillion, and who was our novitiate, and Jo, Fred and myself, a regular Easter
trio, cyclists by choice, yet never averse to any open air form of pleasure
travelling. Jo and Lucy were to share a tent, Tom, Fred and I the other. The
food was communal.

Sadgill is a tiny hamlet of three or four farmhouses nestled deep in the
hills of Eastern Lakeland, just below the head of Long Sleddale, a narrow
ravine served by a lane six miles long from the great highway that climbs
over Shap Fells. Beside the road runs a stream of cascades, pools, and tree-
lined shallows. From its extreme quietness, its lovely situation below the
high fells, yet its accessibility, one would be hard put to it to find a better
starting point for a rambling tour. That is why we chose Sadgill.

We began the ascent of Gatesgarth Pass, the lane losing its character as
such to become a trackway, taking the hillside in a reckless dash, hardly ob-

servant of contours, while the stream on the other side of the tumbledown wall bubbled over the giant steps of many waterfalls into rock-walled pools. Below us now lay Long Sleddale, a green ripple of beauty under brown moorland. From the faultless sky came steady sunshine, and came also the liquid outpourings of the mating curlews, the cries of many pewits. A thousand feet up was a level stretch of sward, a sheep pen, the river, excuse enough to linger, and to camper's eyes, a site for the future.

With leisured steps we left the Pass before its summit, turning up the steep, trackless hillside to the southwest, climbing for an hour or more until we reached a place in the wind, eased off our packs and gazed victoriously over hills and hollows to distant indigo heights, to the tidal sands of the River Leven. The cupped loveliness of Mardale was deep below us. Perhaps we stayed too long at that far-flung view, for, as we started again, the wind pierced, and the warmth was gone from the spring sun. Evening approached.

We walked along the curving ridge of Harter Fell. From the highest summit we saw the fanged teeth of the Langdale peaks, black and startling in the sudden appearance of them above gentler moorland contours. Far below us, at the foot of a chaotic confusion of rock and boulder-stones, pear-shaped Small Water mirrored the sky in a final touch of the desolate. Someone suggested there would be shelter for our tents by the lake, and not too great a height for the cold, so down we plunged, an irregular invasion of half an hour's duration until, from the waterside, we remarked on the towering heights that now stood above.

There was little enough camping ground amongst the wild disorder of rock about the upper end of the tarn, but seasoned campers will see spaces where others would pass unsatisfied, and soon we had our two tents bravely perched on crag-fringed turf. Supper was convivial, taken family-wise, each helping themselves from the common larder, and long into the night the conversation ran.

After the rising of the moon came a change. The wind, at first a booming organ-note on the summits above, shifted, eddied, flung growing gusts into our sanctuary. Small Water blew into squally ripples, the tents flapped, shivered, and after moorings had once broken loose, we placed boulders over the pegs. The moon, herself at first serenely sailing over the reflective lake, now climbed behind hurrying clouds, and when we went to bed the rocky hollow of Small Water was as wild a place of mountain solitude as ever held the tents of venturing ramblers.

In the mountains, the weather changes as rapidly as time. The traveller, knowing these upland moods, is neither surprised nor dismayed, nor is he

AN IMPRESSION OF
LANGDALE.

Fig. 55: An Impression of Langdale

unprepared, but passes on lightheartedly from change to change, for in those infinite variations that lie between sun and storm, day and night, the real beauty of the hills is revealed. Beauty does not only dwell with the sublime; beauty sulks as well as smiles.

From the sunny skies of Good Friday a night of wind lay between the enveloping mists of Easter Saturday morning. The hollow of Small Water was a steaming cauldron pot of rising vapours, now silent and wind-less, the high cliffs invisible, the broken cliffs close by the tents exaggerated beyond reason.

Breakfast, like everything else on that holiday, was a model of communal leisureliness. Not one of us but regarded the change as another phase of mountain grandeur. We packed up late, surprised that, after such a display of appetites, our packs still appeared as bulky as ever, and shouldering them, took to the hills again. We climbed from Small Water by the rocky windings of the Nan Bield Pass, and the pear-shaped lake-let soon disappeared from sight. At the summit of the Pass, already 2,100 ft. high, we turned in a westerly direction along the gently rising plateau of moorland grass that stretches unbroken to the summit of Mardale ill Bell. An Ordnance Survey map and a compass were our guides towards High Street, the aptly named Roman Road which runs south to north on top of the ranges from close by Staveley to Penrith, many glorious miles of breezy summits. Lucy, hearing the name 'High Street', visualised a busy shopping thoroughfare, and promised us ice cream all round upon reaching it. The High Street of Lucy's mind would certainly have been a remarkable example of disconnected ribbon development!

As views go, we saw absolutely nothing for a time. But we saw the encircling mists retreating at our advance, closing behind us, and we felt, even with each other for company, the utter solitude that bound the hills and ourselves. Eventually a wall displayed the hand of man, and crossing it we soon reached the ribbon of greensward which betrayed the Roman Road, a triumph, we thought, of map and compass reading. We turned northward, Lucy pondering quietly upon another shattered illusion.

We were close to the edge of a precipice of some sort, for great hanging cornices of snow, the last surviving fragments of a long, bitter winter, stretched over the gully-heads. Then came a sudden gust which tore the mists, revealing to us the depths of a desolate valley holding the white sheet of Hayes Water. We looked through a hole in the mist as with the eyes of a hovering bird, yet even as we watched the gap closed again. But the wind was rising. Sometimes the brown side of a mountain would stand before us for a moment, sometimes the tarn, and sometimes the whole span of the treeless dale far beneath. The mists returned less frequently, until finally they retreated to greater heights, and left our distance dully clear. As we trod the way the Legions had made, wondering what their exiled eyes had seen, what their thoughts were, our eyes surveying the distant glens and the indistinct greenery of Patterdale far away, our senses exulted; we sang and

Fig. 56: Angle Tarn

spoke without thought, and thought without speech. We were five individual minds with a singular oneness, each with his own interpretation. In time
we made our way down to a crystal stream besides which we dined. For
drink, the mountain water! We did not consider the time – we were hungry,
therefore we ate! There was heavy-going bog in our next move across a
wide stretch of tangly heather and marsh grass. We joined sheep-tracks,
leaving them at will, with but a general direction, careless of everything
about us but the hills, ever changing, a reflection of the unsettled sky
above.

There came a heavy drizzle of rain, while we wound about a region of
lovely turf and outcropped rock to Angle Tarn, an irregular lake abounding
in perfect nooks for camping, and dreamy swimming water, with shores
worthy of an estuary, delightful heathery islets. Angle Tarn, skirted in the
drizzle, was captivating. Eventually we looked down on Ullswater at the
Patterdale end. Brothers Water was directly below us, Kirkstone Pass
wriggled up its narrow ravine in a white thread. Over Helvellyn the grey
mists curled. The rain ceased, the wind fell, and for half an hour before descending to Ullswater, we lazed comfortably in the mild atmosphere while
the sun strove to break through.

Three of the party went down to the nearest farm to secure our breakfast
eggs, while Jo and I meandered along the track that passes a glorious
lakeside campsite we had often used. We sheltered from a final shower un-

der resinous, dripping spruce, and played with a foraging foxhound, a lean, beautiful creature with soft brown eyes which quite belied its hunting nature. Its loping, easy movements were a pleasure to watch. The party united again, we sauntered along, beauty in our eyes all the time, now the varied loveliness of the east side of Ullswater, ever-changing as the path traversed rocky places; places of thin, hillside birch woods; places where streams came rushing down little dells. Ullswater too, placid under the clearing sky, its isles reflected topsy-turvy with all their charming loads of colour. Six miles along, when we were pleasantly tired, we came to a tumbling beck below a waterfall, with restful banks of springy turf. There we stopped and set up our outfits quite early in the evening.

We splashed about half naked, in a zeal of scrubbing.... *"Dipping tired feet in some cool-flowing brook"*, as Jo fittingly quoted. On such a day it was meet that we should stop in good time, lest, crowding ourselves out with too much beauty seen, we fail to enjoy a single moment. And how sumptuously we dined!

Jo and I, refreshed and un-sated, climbed a low eminence to watch the moon arise over the hills, casting a long, golden ripple along the water. There was the peace of perfect tranquillity amongst the hills on that golden Easter evening.

By the obvious subterfuge of putting our watches forward one hour, Tom and I managed to persuade the rest to rise earlier next morning. There were suspicions, but nobody was averse to the advantage once they were out of bed, for an hour gained is a gain indeed. This time our rucksacks packed more comfortably, and after a final gambol in the stream, we slung them up. A moment later another grand campsite passed into the land of the remembered. Shortly we reached the hamlet of Sandwick, where the lane along the lowest reach of Ullswater from Pooley Bridge comes to its end. For about a mile we tramped this lane by a stream where kingfishers skimmed, fly-catching, and over which trees bent their blossoms. At a fork, an insignificant path beguiled us over a bracken covered hill straight down into the quiet seclusion of Martindale.

Lucy cast a shoe heel. Unknown to us she had suffered torture with her shoes, which, flimsy, high-ish heeled, were more suited to the High Street of her illusion than that of reality. But realising it too late, she suffered in silence, and only the sight of torn feet brought us the realisation. Despite initial and painful mistakes, of such stuff are true ramblers made. With his usual ingenuity, Tom made a very good roadside repair, and overhauled the shoes as well, clinching many in-pointed nails.

The route we preferred slanted upwards in easy stages, on a well defined track. We had many a halt to survey the sweep of the dale below, with its cultivated, wall-bound fields, neatly laid out farms, and, showing beyond the end of the road, the last, shining reach of Ullswater. On the ridge we looked into another deep dale which closed abruptly before us, and walking round the head of it, faced a steep wall of brown and green moorland. Along the top of this lay High Street. At a green spot by a ruined farmhouse we drank moorland water, and then sauntered upwards in a steady slant along paths of our own making, finally reaching a snow cornice at the summit. A gentle upwards tilt brought us to a wall – the same long division wall of yesterday – sheltering the Roman Road. As we ate our dry lunch, snugly sheltered, we looked down on Bampton and the foot of Haweswater; down a rumpled dale; over the far-flung, dappled country of the Border, even to that great Pennine barricade, Cross Fell.

Our walk led us round the head of Martindale Common, where warning notices bespoke a deer-preserve, to the peak of High Seat[10], 2,634 ft., with its stones bleached white. The views into the Lakeland massif were superb, flung across the western sky. Helvellyn summit still nursed the mists, but Striding Edge was clear, seeming a knife poised in an upward swoop. The sunless sky was settled, almost windless, and the air was cool and clear.

A descent to Mardale, over stream, moor, and down rocky screes where cascades leapt, occupied an hour, and all the time the gorgeous valley unfolded, with the silver spread of Haweswater at our feet, untouched yet by the Waterworks scheme[11]. There was an accommodating farm at Mardale Green, where great enamel jugs of tea were forthcoming ad lib at our request, and a green space where we laid a grand spread.

The next stage of our journey lay into little-rambled country, over the ancient corpse track to Swindale. Along this old right-of-way were shouldered the coffins of the dead farm-folks, for burial at Mardale. What a fully alive, glorious evening it was on the hills again, with views, lovely turf to the feet, and the fine thrill of new country! We descended from the quiet moors to Swindale Head with its one farm, a place of serene beauty and tranquillity, which entered into our hearts. Near the ultimate end of the dale, we crossed a causeway below which an extensive marsh clearly told of a lake-let in heavy weather, then climbed to the open moor, by a ravine in the depth of which a tiny river bawled lustily, the child of an erstwhile thundering waterfall. From that point onwards we agreed that we were fortunate indeed to strike a dry season, for otherwise our passage would have been tremendously difficult with bog. We reached Mosedale – surely Des-

---

10   High Raise?
11   To further flood the valley and pipe the water to Manchester.

olation under another name, the oldest desolation in the world, that of heaving wastes of moor and bog, trackless, treeless, untouched by the hand of man, and serving only to offer a lonely wandering ground for black-faced sheep. We have seen such places before, by the headwaters of Maize Beck on Cross Fell; by Geldie Burn below the Cairngorms; on Rannoch Moor, and not far from Hull Pot, near Ribblehead, to mention a few coming at random to mind. They are the very basis of the primeval world.

We forked into Little Mosedale, if anything even wilder. Then we sighted a stony track by a stream, following it. There were some small worked-out quarries higher up, broken gates on the way, and finally, in a nook below the merging of fell and dale, the deserted summer dwellings, Mosedale Cottages, a blank, forlorn pair of stone houses. Occasionally one comes across those buildings in places which are quite uninhabitable during the winter. For one brief season each summer the farmer and his family bring their simplest stores and the bare moorland huts become a hive of activity when the sheep are rounded up and the shearing begins. In the Highlands and on the Hebridean islands these type of places are more common, and are called 'summer shielings'.

We nursed a tiny hope as we approached Mosedale Cottages. Jo had heard of a thirsty rambler calling for a drink one day, and being plied with such quantities of potent, home brewed ale that he fell asleep on the rough couch and did not awaken until the clock had made the double circuit. Alas! we were more than a month too early!

So we tramped on, now a little tired, promising ourselves a grand supper when we fixed up camp. Soon the two cottages and all other signs of human effort were out of sight, and on the virgin moor we climbed through a wide, shallow pass. The air grew chilly, the sky became leaden in aspect, and where a hush of broody quiet had prevailed, was now a growing wind with menace in its tone. Once more the mood of the hills was changing, a storm was imminent.

For a long time we walked, not comfortably, over stubbly sod, through rank marsh, descending at last, dog tired, and in the dusk, to the sheep-pen, a thousand feet up Gatesgarth Pass. The circuit was complete.

As we had often promised ourselves on the long, hungry crossing over Mosedale, we made a final supper, into which we concentrated most of the food and all our remaining delicacies. Far into the night we sang songs – happily overheard by none save the fearful sheep huddled in the windy, outer darkness. As we made up our beds the long-threatened rain beat down upon the little tents, a steady, drumming symphony, easing us into slumber.

On the waking senses, drummed the rain. Dry and securely cosy, yet the

" Softly the evening came. The sun from the western horizon   *Evening in the*

Like a magician extends his golden wand o'er the landscape;'   *Kentmere Valley.*

—Longfellow.

Fig. 57: Evening in the Kentmere Valley

sounding patter of rain close to the ears, is a sensation which every camper is accustomed to. It is a pleasant sound to be awakened by, and a man never feels more supremely comfortable than in those few drowsy minutes before full alertness arrives. Perhaps it is at such times, when outside conditions are so distasteful, and inside conditions are so airily delightful, that man is at his happiest.

In plain truth, Easter Monday morning was distinctly wet. Over everything clung the obscuring mists. A late, lingering breakfast, a lazy discussion, a little leg-pulling, and the rain had ceased. Wet tents were packed, and a little regretfully we tramped down the Pass, beside the cascading stream now swollen into a noisy torrent, back to Sadgill Farm where the contents of five rucksacks were spilled and repacked into panniers and saddlebags. Once again we were awheel, the motorcycle with Lucy clinging onto its pillion for dear life, jolting ahead down the narrow lane to order lunch at a house near Kendal. The day brightened as we rode down Long Sleddale, and slowly the mists steamed off the hills of our ramblings. Lunch passed merrily enough, and in sunshine we joined the traffic stream, our faces set for home.

The experiment had proved its worth, and had opened for us an even more free mode of travel in the hills than that provided by the bicycles. A careful choice of the lightest of equipment, an elimination of unnecessary extras, sufficient food, and one is free to go anywhere without regard for the coming of night and the seeking of accommodation, with the restraints which that implies.

We had chosen our country wisely too. That neglected portion of Eastern Lakeland lying between Ullswater and Shap Fells contains some rare gems for the seeker, and, at such a popular holiday as Easter, did not show us a single other rambler!

Christmas, 1939.

Fig. 58: Christmas in Craven

Christmas 1939

The weak sun of winter made a good setting as we climbed Sawley Brow. Below us the Ribble coiled along its rich valley into the near haze about Clitheroe – ahead the dusk and Gisburn for tea.

Now the chilly eve, a shadowy road violently undulating, ludicrously dimmed lamps. The first winter of war; the first black-out. How strangely dead the villages of the Skipton road, all shuttered and sleeping, though the hour was barely 6 pm. Ahead, a bus ghoulishly lighted, took aboard a quiet crowd of people, and moved on, bound for the town. With one more day to Christmas Eve, Skipton should have been a blaze of light, a hive of noisy activity. But the lights of Skipton were quenched, and with them the spirits of the crowd. The crowd was there – the torches flickered, but the people shuffled along in a hum of half silence. What a strange War this was, a War of silence and darkness, with a thousand towns all a-gloom and great, inactive armies sat silently behind their barricades, a War of dark threats, dark portends, dark expectancy. In truth the clouds were gathering!

We turned our tandem northwards towards the Dales, the welcome crescent of a rising moon bringing lighter patches, deeper shadows over the fair face of the land. Past the old house of the strange name, Nonegoby, and beside Rylstone Fell, surely haunted this night if ever it was, by the White Doe so dramatised by Wordsworth.

"The bright moon sees that valley small
Where Rylstone's old sequestered Hall
A venerable image yields
Of quiet to the neighbouring fields;"

Nothing now remains but a bare tracing near the village, of "Rylstone's old sequestered Hall", and the lonely hunting tower of the Nortons is now gone from the face of the earth. In the Rising of the North, in November 1569, the ancient prophesy of the fate of the Nortons came to pass, and death and desolation was their share of the spoil. Even the bells of Rylstone Church carried the inscribed legend, and played *"Their Sabbath music – God us Ayde"*! This was the night for such old stories to be remembered, and Jo and I searched our memories for old tales of the Nortons as we rode steadily past the lovely old village and swept down by Cracoe to Thresh-field in Wharfedale. For Jo, at least, half the pleasure of the ride thereafter was lost with the discovery of ice on the road, and careless swoop became sober crawl down the gritty edge of many a fine hill. From the great bulge of Kilnsey Crags we climbed, and crept safely down to Kettlewell. A final labour to the knoll where stands an old chapel, at that time the youth hostel. Our ride was over. Great fires gave cheer to the damp, half derelict place. A hostel of the Spartan type, Kettlewell attracted only the enthusiasts willing to fend for themselves, the real, solid core of the great movement. At such places everyone is at once a chum – everyone starts level and remains so. At Miss Jacques cosy cottage away down in the village, some few might get their breakfast, but most of us were self-cookers, and experts with the misused primus stoves in the lean-to kitchen.

We were at once friends (some were not strangers to us); our beds were claimed, our suppers made, and cyclists tales were repeated under the slowly airing blankets, a great circle of us about the fire. Later in the even-ing someone made tea to keep the stories circulating, then quietly, as the embers died, one after another sought their beds until a handful of us re-mained, smoking, talking, listening, a rambler on a thousand hills, a pot-holer of note, a traveller in many lands, a lover of quiet English corners.

The Christmas Eve was a Sabbath day in 1939. In Kettlewelldale morn-ing was mild and calm, the roads and roofs wet with a relaxation of the light frost. Most of the hostellers, including ourselves, had booked for three nights, and we went our several ways with promises to meet again at even-ing. Jo and I had decided to explore, in more leisurely fashion than usual, the greater part of Wharfedale, first down the west side of the river, then back on the other side. There are excellent roads on each side, and

Fig. 59: Kilnsey Crag

Wharfedale, like most of the Yorkshire Dales, is packed with variety. It is, I think, as rich in fertility and historical interest, as any green strath in the land.

We crossed the sloping bridge and climbed until Kettlewell lay beneath, its old houses straddling the broad strath, the river, tree-lined, smooth and shallow. Farther down the dale the bold crag of Kilnsey bulged outward. We rode slowly past this very familiar, yet remarkable feature, one of the distinctive features of Craven. Half a mile long, 165 ft. at its highest point, its great outward bulge makes it quite unclimbable, though it can easily be reached from the steep Mastiles Lane, which runs beside its southern flank. Apparently it is close to the road, but if the local youths wager that you can't hit it with a stone thrown from the road, don't take them on.

The tiny nestling village with its old inn, the 'Tennant Arms' – you should see the old, worn panelling in the spacious-windowed dining room – is steeped in antiquity. Domesday book calls it "Chilesie", and not long after the Book was compiled, the monks of Fountains Abbey, acquiring the great fells to the west – still called Fountains Fell – drove their flocks to Kilnsey for the annual shearing. And to this day Kilnsey Show is held in the early days of September. Even yet the shepherd dominates the cosy hamlet below the Crag. The road, approaching Threshfield, climbs into woodland, the river entering the gorge of Ghaistrills, and as one reaches the summit one sees backward views of the tapering dale and its bright river.

The map marks a waterfall where the road and river are nearest, but we have only found a small cascade which could never attain that dignity. Threshfield, quiet and grey, with the slow river meandering under its old Dales bridge, and its ancient stories, one of which tells of straggling Scots in the '45 hiding in a cave. The abundant caves of these limestone hills must, after all, have sheltered many a fugitive. Again one's mind turns to the Nortons and Wordsworth;

> *"In Craven's wilds is many a den, to shelter persecuted men:*
> *For underground is many a cave, where they might lie, as in the grave,*
> *Until this storm hath ceased to rave:"*

A peaceful place that's had its past, and now dreams on it in sheltered nooks. And ancient Linton, home of author Halliwell Sutcliffe, Wharfedales greatest lover. There is a curious bridge here called Redmayne Bridge, built three hundred years ago, specially narrow in the centre to stop the farmers from sneaking their carts over, and Little Emily's Bridge near the Mill, again recall Wordsworth's tale of the Nortons. To know Linton however, one must turn to "The Striding Dales" and absorb the atmosphere transported into print by Sutcliffe. Again, tiny Thorpe-in-the-Hollow. Constantly one must turn aside to hidden hamlets grown old with the hills.

Still high above the river, we come to Burnsall. The lovely old village straggles down the hill to the river. Again there is a bridge, grown into its surround, and as strong and graceful as ever after its hundreds of years of life. The church stands high, on the main road; we watched the last of the worshippers leaving after morning service, then roamed the place at will, finding there relics from a past incredibly distant. Remains of crosses of Saxon origin, over a thousand years old, a font of early Norman times, of sculptures of the Adoration, a venerable place indeed it is, impregnated with generations upon generations of hardy dales folk, to so very many of whom it christened, wed and sheltered on the way to their last meeting place, just outside. Next to the churchyard – best seen from there – is a gem of Elizabethan master-building, the Grammar School. Some aver that it is the finest of its kind in all England. And then the two grey old rectories, facing each other across the road, with their 'squint' windows so built that the occupants of each might watch the other without themselves being seen. One wonders why the rivalry? Relics again, from stealthy, suspicious times.

In truth Wharfedale was showing us its rare treasures on this mild, sunny Christmas Eve. A short ride into deep woodland and then great grey Barden Tower came in view. Freely we rambled about the roofless, melan-

'....the shy recess...Of Barden's lowly quietness.' Wordsworth.

Fig. 60: Barden Tower

choly ruin, raised above the broad green pasture, and amid the soundless walls took imaginative peeps into a not too warlike past. Perhaps the fierce name of the Cliffords, lords of this part of Craven was enough to ward off marauders, though there is called to mind, one, captive for years in the Cumbrian hills, came into his own under the title of "Shepherd Lord" Clifford. The Tower was twice ruined. That lady of doubtful virtue, Lady Anne Clifford, Countess of Dorset, Pembroke and Montgomery, restored it in 1657, and used it on occasion during her restless wanderings about her huge domain.

The sweeping road, high in the woods above the river, swung round a great loop down to Bolton Abbey on its tongue of land formed by the Wharfe in one of its spacious and gracious positions. Once again we dip into Wordsworth, whose *"White Doe of Rylstone"* immortalises the legend of its foundation. This actually occurred in 1151, when the monks of Embsay, a few miles nearer Skipton, deserted the poor buildings and began their long and fruitful existence. Perhaps those father and son legends are glorified into 'truth' by long useage, but they are happily apt and need not be explored too closely. This one concerns the young "Boy of Egremont" (named for his birthplace in Cumberland) who, while jumping across the narrow Strid in Bolton Woods, was thrown into the turgid water by a hesitant hound, whose leash was twined in his hand.

The boy was drowned, and the sorrowing mother endowed the Abbey as a memory to him. Wordsworth records the dramatic moment when the falconer brought home the dead child, asking: *"What is good for a bootless bene?"* The mother replied: *"Endless weeping",* and sought consolation in the dedication of the Priory. In its northern position, its magnificence and wealth drew the raiding Scots like a magnet, and time and again it was pillaged. Time and again it arose still more magnificent, even though under the austere control of the order of St Augustine. The monks sang and flourished, many hundreds of freemen as well as villains toiled, were dependent upon them, and for over four hundred years there were built exquisite architectural gems in every period, only lovely fragments of which remain to us. On that pleasant Christmas Eve when the Wharfe ran quietly past the stepping stones, and the long nave was left to its own broodings, we found a charm never known in the hot, crowded glare of summer.

There is, too, the legend of the White Doe, which year by year, on a certain Sabbath, finds her way over the hills from Rylstone to rest upon the grave of Francis Norton, the last of the male line, who perished after his eight sons in the ill-fated Pilgrimage of Grace (the Rising of the North). How quiet the narrow road past the ancient Hall to the aged hamlet of Bolton Bridge. We joined the Skipton road for a short distance to a quarry, the entrance to which lies under the railway line. In this quarry is laid open a fine example of how mountain ranges are formed, and this particular face is preserved for geological study. The strata is crumpled laterally and in tangential form, best described, as I've read somewhere by compressing sideways a pile of cloths. If enough pressure is applied the layers will be wrinkled and folded. In the same way the strata, first laid horizontally, were severely stressed until they lie in every angle to the vertical, yet still

Fig. 61: Cloister Doorway, Bolton Abbey

retaining their strata, and one can follow the arched bend of limestone, millstone grit, and Silurian, in turns.

The short, bright day was already beginning to darken as we returned past the old Priory, now hurrying to add one more sight while daylight remained. A footpath led down through steeply sloping woods of oak and ash to the river again, at the Strid, that "Striding place" of rough rock-walls where the river churns beneath and the smooth slippery rocks tempt one to cross. So easy to cross – so easy to slip – and to meet a certain watery grave as did the legendary "Boy" of long ago, and many others, more recent, more authentic. As we walked back through the woods the day was done; under the trees the shadows were already deep. In half a mile we joined a cycling club at tea, a real modern Yorkshire tea, as good as any the Cliffords' ever commanded.

Now the night was almost black. We crossed steeply sloping Barden Bridge, to pursue our return journey on the eastern side of Wharfedale. In daylight the swinging roads and string of villages on that side will hold the enquirer equally in time and interest. There is great enjoyment on mild nights on not too-familiar roads with nothing else to keep one's watch, and we rode our steady measure to the tyres, humming between steep hedges, past black woodland, round quaint edges of drowsy hamlets, Howgill, Appletreewick, the near glint of the river, the outward swing to Hebden, then almost provincial Grassington, and the last, narrower, more winding, stone-walled miles by Conistone to Kettlewell.

From our Knoll, where stands the Hostel, we looked out after supper. Brilliant moonlight lighted a scene of frosty beauty, with all the roof-tops a-glitter and the grass dusty with fine hoar. Then back to our songs and tales and the great fire.

Fig. 62: Grassington Bridge

The sober minded Hostel party quickly tidied up house this Christmas morning, eager, all of us, to spend the day on the road, or the fells. We bolted the door as the bells were ringing their merry peals – the last Christmas bells for three wild years, had we known it – and began a walk cumride up the narrow dale flanked by Great Whernside. At the foot of Park Rash we overtook the plodding postman who gladly delayed his bulging delivery at the one house in the valley-head to talk, the while his terrier reenacted many a remembered chase. Then a tramping pair from the Hostel came up, and the four of us hauled the tandem up the mad capers of the road. On the long, lifting summit at 1,652 ft., this was a grand spring day of golden sunshine, with not a trace of snow or winter frost, even on 2,310 ft. Great Whernside, which rarely in winter fails to hold a white crown. Our companions took to the heather for the distant poll of Buckden Pike; we crossed Great Hunters Stone, the turfy track wriggling down in loops and twists to the deep head of Coverdale. There, beside the small arch over the river Cover was our camping patch, and there the road leading up to Hunters Hall where, getting on for seven years before, Jo, in a quest for the morning milk, had arrived just in time to practice midwifery to the mistress of the house who was alone with her pains. Perhaps it would have been fitting to carry a Christmas greeting to the folks there, but we moved on, and now it is more than likely the goodwife will never know who was the timely benefactress. The tiny hamlets of little Coverdale, all elbows jutting out on the narrow road, were passed – Bradley, Horsehouse, then the long straggly village of the straggly name, Carlton Coverdale, at the further edge of which we branched left and came at once to the hamlet, fork-road, and inn, of Melmerby, all set at the edge of a moor. Though it was Christmas Day, our request for tea at the inn was smilingly agreed upon, and I'll be prepared to swear that the children were hurriedly moved from a cosy parlour for our benefit. The warm fire and the toys remained!

We climbed high over Middleham Moor, the steep trough of Coverdale behind us, ahead a gracious section of Wensleydale, and zig-zagged steeply down into the quaint, single street of West Witton. Where the road reached the level bed of the dale we dumped the tandem and along a path skirting field and thin scrub, reached Aysgarth Falls. In the mile or so of wooded gorge traversed by the River Ure from Aysgarth to this point are three fine cascades, this the lowest, being the best of them. The river has cut great steps in its bed, with fine effect, and a little scrambling about the rocks – "jostling for position" – gives some lovely glimpses of the tumbling waters. From the topmost slabs, looking down towards the calmer meanders below one gets a fair idea of the great, unsuspected descent of the terrain.

Fig. 63: Aysgarth Falls

When we reached the road again the sun was setting, and the sky a wonderful scene of delicate colouring from vivid red to the palest of green. For quite a time we stood upon the road watching, until the dusk had quenched the translucence, and deepest blue to starry black appeared.

We rode into Bishopdale now, our brief acquaintance with Yoredale sufficing, and finding nowhere to obtain tea for our sandwiches at West Burton, were well content with a snug roadman's shelter just beyond the village.

Thereafter the warming influence of the long gradual climb up the shallowing dale to its final steep pitches of Kidstones Pass; the easy sweeps down from the watershed, past Cray of the Little Waterfall to Old Buckden, and the easy miles of Wharfeside lane to Kettlewell again, in ample time to join our remaining supplies with others for our Christmas Supper.... and the wee drappie which, by common consent, once in a year relaxes a stern Youth Hostel rule.

Came the last morning of the short holiday, and the hostel, spick and span, was locked up, goodbyes said, and a final chat with Miss Jacques, the benevolent warden, to who the hostel was almost purely a labour of love. The air was mild and sunny, the river sparkled, the whole atmosphere was like an early morning in Spring, as we wheeled towards Kilnsey with another tandem pair from Morley. Where green Littondale opened to the North, we bade our friends goodbye, turned through a gate leading onto a patch of macadam over the pasture – an improbable looking sort of road, and soon came to tiny Hawkswick, the hamlet that dreams away undisturbed by the softly flowing, tree-lined Skirfare. And then we reached Arncliffe, the "Capital" of Littondale. At Arncliffe is a most spacious green about which the whole village clusters, and every house has grown into its place. At the foot of the village where Cowside Beck flows down to the

Fig. 64: Owlcotes, Littondale

river, the pasturage is open to the moor. We looked in the old church by the river, and found the interior much restored. There was, however, proudly displayed by the side of the Great War memorial, another, much older, containing the names of the 30 men of Littondale who fought at Flodden Field in 1513. The names are of families that live in Littondale today, and in many cases their descendants must be farming the same land, and living on the same sites. Beside each name is given the manner of arms carried, and whether mounted. Thus we read *"John Metcalfe, a bille, Will Johnson, a bowe"* etc. Littondale is full of venerable houses and manors, and in Arncliffe are two of the loveliest, Bridge House, over the bridge and across the river from the church, with a beautiful garden sloping down to the water, and Owlcotes, just up the dale. "Owlcotes" is a supreme example of stone Tudor architecture. It is more; it is a symphony in stone, it is, we are sure, the most beautiful house in the Dales.

So we left tree-embowered Arncliffe with its ageless, grey beauty, all Tudor and Georgian and village green, and Flodden memories – even its literary corners, for at Bridge House has stayed Charles Kingsley and Halliwell Sutcliffe, and turned up the Dale, now wilder and narrower to tiny Litton with its old inn, and quaint old Hall. There are people in the Dale who refuse to acknowledge the present name of Littondale, and always use the more pastoral, and older, Arnerdale. Yes, Arnerdale runs easily from the tongue, it smacks of the "tofts" of their Norse forbears, like the old sheep numerals that people say are still used far up the dale at Foxup and Cosh. We will come back to Arnerdale!

We joined a green road which crossed a dry river by a high arch. Yes a dry riverbed. We went looking for the Skirfare, which we found flowing placidly a few yards below. A little higher up we found it, too, quite a strong flow! But about the bridge, the great limestone slabs, worn into potholes and fissures, were bone-dry. We were of course in the heart of Craven, where these caprices are not uncommon, and remind one of a sub-terranean Craven, as wonderful as that above. Our green road climbed steeply beside a wall. Over the wall the ground fell away to the terraced depths of Pen-y-Ghent Ghyll, with the tiny farms of Hesleden in the delta below, and Littondale closing in beyond, at Halton Ghyll, overlorded by huge moorlands. From Halton Ghyll a coiling road advanced along the other side of Pen-y-Ghent Ghyll, and on a wide turfy moor our green track joined it. There was a final swing, and we were on the summit, at 1,430 ft.

Silverdale Road is one of the finest in Craven, running through a broad and deep pass between Pen-y-Ghent and Fountains Fell. On the summit it is unfenced, and the moor is spacious and turfy, with Pen-y-Ghent curving grandly to its whale-backed summit. Pen-y-Ghent is almost supreme in Yorkshire: like Ingleborough it is an isolated hill, and is inspiring viewed from any angle. It possesses that rare quality of being comely to look upon, a fine hill to climb, and when climbed shows views worthwhile. And, like Ingleborough, its underground marvels are paramount. The environs of Pen-y-Ghent are our finest weekend playgrounds, and they are not neglected. At Dale Head our road passed through a gate and began to dip into Silverdale, a deepening valley quite barren, with terraces of limestone slicing the brown and green moor. As one gets lower a backward glance reveals the sharp prow of Pen-y-Ghent towering above all, impelling the wandering eye. The road is better now-a-days, and one can stare around with caution until the final steep slide directly down to Stainforth-in-Ribblesdale.

We had a very good lunch in Settle. The rest of the story is of an afternoon saunter across the Forest of Bowland, a dusky ride into the Ribble Valley, a quiet tea close by the ancient Abbey at Whalley, and home again by dark, familiar lanes.

It sometimes happens that, in the heart of winter there comes a single day which seems to have become detached from its rightful place somewhere in April, and its beauty shines all the more against the grey tones which surround it. So it was this Christmas, and not a single day but four,

Fig. 65: Winter at Beddgelert

incredibly bright and serene. Neither could we have chosen a more fitting frame to mirror them, than the country of Craven, with its great moors and shining scars, its long green dales, unspoilt and populous with proud relics of a past which has not been too bitter. The things that count live on in its people, kindliness and hospitality; with these things, and with the good earth that has always nourished them they will survive many ages yet.

Annalong.
—What's in a Name?

I travelled down from Belfast town,
  By sea-fringed strand I ran along
Where mountain slopes come sweeping down
  To meet the waves at Annalong.

    To Annalong I ran along;
    The lilting name of Annalong
    I sang to every man along
    The swinging road to Annalong!

There is no fame of ancient name,
  No promenade to scan along;
And no-one wished, who ever came,
  To linger long in Annalong

    To Annalong I ran along—
    The striding road to Annalong.
    Fly along, fan along,
    Hie along to Annalong!

The big ships ride on Belfast tide,
  They count the world their span along,
While hugging close the harbour side.
  The little ships of Annalong.

    To Annalong I ran along,
    Sing a song of Annalong!
    Play along, plan along,
    Plod along to Annalong!

Now I proclaim—what's in a name,
  That sends me fast as can along?
It could not ever be the same
  When once I'd looked on Annalong.

    To Annalong I ran along—
    The magic name of Annalong!
    Lim-along, lan-along,
    Lone-along to Annalong!

PENNINE
COUNTERBLAST.

` The marvellous mugs, miraculous mugs,

The mystical mugs we are `
`Ballode of St Barbara:`   Chesterton

Y.G. 8. 1931.

It was in our minds to revisit an eccentric old lady at Peckett Well, in the direction of Keighley. Fred and I had met her in November 1930, in the course of a run in the Haworth country; she kept a small sweet shop in a cottage on the moors, and served cups of tea as a sideline. Although quite a dear old dame, she had become afflicted with a most primitive kind of religious mania, and when she had rather frugally served our tea, the good woman started on the most fervent discourse. Apparently she had convinced herself that heaven had sent us, ripe for conversion. We listened with dutiful silence and profound admiration at the flow of quotations, which hopelessly damned every other religious sect, and condemned all modern innovations as vehicles of the devil, but the only thing we became convinced of at the end of a two hours' sermon was that she was becoming, in her old age, an introvert.

So we arranged for a party of us to repeat the ordeal. The road between Bolton and Rochdale, via Bury and Jericho, covers thirteen miles; and of those ten miles have setts and tram lines. The next four to Littleborough have also tramlines and setts, which are at their worst, and that is bad! Seven of us climbed Blackstone Edge in heavy rain – it had rained all the morning – and stopped at the Shepherd's Rest on the way for coffee, which was poured from a great jug into generous cups ad-lib. From the summit of Blackstone Edge the usual views were smothered in rain-clouds, through which snowy crests showed faintly white. Speckled with snow, the russet moors down to Cragg looked grand, but Mytholmroyd[12] brought industrialism into the valley which must have had it's beauty once, all the way to

---

12 Pronounced 'Momroyd'.

Hebden Bridge. From there, a two mile tramp up to wet, windy moorlands, with the winter-stripped woods of Golden Valley below took us to Peckett Well, and the old lady's cottage.

After lunch our hostess, having again persuaded herself that we had been specially sent, gathered us round like a Sunday School class, and for nearly three hours held forth on the wickedness of the world, and the heavenly warmth that permeated The Brethren. We were exhorted to give up our ways of life, including cycling, particularly on Sundays, not even to ride on buses, and by closely following the Path which the Lord had personally revealed to her, we might expect to dwell, not in the halls of the Chosen, but in, say, a tiny sheep-pen far down the scale. It was quite natural that she would inherit a substantial part of the Kingdom, who had been so good all her life, and we, who were starting late, would have to be content with a small apartment almost, but not quite in, the Outer Void. When she put in the bit about giving up cycling there was a startled look about us; that, we thought, was going too far, and there was a definite reaction, a kind of hardening of our hearts. We began to feel a conviction that perhaps after all, this world of sinners is preferable to the tinselled emptiness of weary immortality. As Mark Twain put it, *"her statements are interesting, but tough"*. We got bored and were glad to plunge into the wild conditions which reigned outside.

One of the two Freds departed for home and a patiently waiting sweetheart. It was well for him that he did! The rest of us, eyes glued on the map, joined a tenth class road that struck across a ravine. The lane had, however, long been claimed as private property, and in consequence we had obstacles to cross, wire fences, ploughed land, and stone walls. No obstacle, however, has yet barred our way. A hillside road we found was bad and snowbound, but it led along some fine moors to the valley road that runs up from Walshaw Dene, a gorgeous bit of river scenery, with the streams in flood. At a fork-road we chose the left one, a new looking road, under the impression that it was the Longcauseway, leading to Burnley, and ran into the teeth of the wind. After two miles of slogging we fetched up dead in the midst of the huge, half finished Gorple waterworks scheme. The road had only been built for the scheme. By that time it was 5.10 pm., and we had all acquired ravenous appetites, but we were determined not to go back. A workman mumbled some hazy directions, as a result of which we struck across a forest of railway lines, over many improvised bridges, and simultaneous with nightfall, arrived in the middle of a vast, churned up claybed, the very bed of the reservoir-to-be. We struggled over the awful morass, sometimes on our necks, until we were daubed all over with yellow clay, somehow keeping the bikes with us, and at last, by good luck, reached a road leading out of it. In two more miles this road, which had sunk to the level of a miserable track, came to a full stop amongst a collection of log huts, pipes and steelwork, the upper part of the huge scheme.

The outlook was extremely unhealthy. Our hunger had got us where we needed to be strongest – at the knees – the wind swept across in a sort of savage glee at it's six shivering playthings; the rain battered in like a whip, and all the daylight was spent. Dark bulky moorland with rocks on the easterly summits hulked up in the gloom like grotesque fantastics in a world of

"We were glad to plunge into the wild conditions outside."

Fig. 66: "We were glad to plunge into the wild conditions outside"

unreality.

It didn't occur to us to light our lamps, the poor glimmers from the cheap oil lamps we used at that time could hardly have helped us anyway. Somebody discovered a track or a stream – I think it was a bit of both, so we all followed, strung out like sheep, and got thoroughly soaked from the thighs down, and from the thighs up. Eventually a farm building loomed black and ruinous, we trooped through the deserted yard and along another track which took us on to something faintly resembling a road. This was the Widdop Cross-Worsthorne road, locally called the Gorple road, but none of us knew that, we just tramped on, still in single file like sheep, but joking, perhaps an unconscious attempt to keep our spirits up. I have noticed time and again that tendency to laugh in the face of adversity. Hopes of an early tea had gone, yet blithely we lied about the warm, cosy room awaiting us in the nearest hamlet, though we suspected the probability of getting just the opposite.

A real river came on to the road, and for a long way kept there; we

'We struggled over the awful morass.'

Fig. 67: "We struggled over the awful morass"

dimly saw the water, heard it's chattering beneath our feet as we waded along it. Our clothing dripped to the last stitch, yet we still thought life funny, while Jo, the only woman present, took her part like a man, reacting finely under such impossible conditions. The one saving stimulus was laughter. The condition of the road was shocking, piled with slushy snow-drifts, dissected by water, and lower down a mere heap of stones. At last we saw light ahead, and descended into Worsthorne at 6.50 pm.

We found a warm cabin where tea, hot pies and peas were served to us, and even the wooden forms and trestle tables were as velvet stalls in the dining halls of heaven. Nobody complained. The day was hopeless, the project mad, causing at least one physical collapse, a fight with pneumonia, but we emerged neither sadder nor wiser. At Peckett Well pearls of wisdom had been cast before us, a chosen path had been outlined for us, but we chose our own and it had proved a Pennine Counterblast. Even now it has not occurred to us to fulfil the first condition. We have chosen our path, lead where it will!

Fig. 68: "I saw a vision set in virgin white"

Fig. 69: The Triple-headed Breieldens

Easter 1936

Easter morning, and early awheel on Cheshire roads. A fine wind abaft, well ahead of the traffic, a lovely, sunny morning, and Jo and Fred, and I, tandem, single, and camping kits. There seems to be no holiday like Easter, the first of the year, with its bright promise of Spring, and later, dalliance days. Seeking always something new at Easter, some new directions, we had decided, after the usual luxurious period of hesitation, to turn our wheels towards Shropshire. Much of Shropshire was new ground.

Our first meal was just within the borders, at a small cottage on the outskirts of Whitchurch. The streets of the market town were already becoming thronged by purposeful motorists whose chief aim seemed to be in speeding westwards into Wales or north for the Lancashire coast. There are two excellent roads to Shrewsbury, the main road via Prees Heath and Wem, and the more meandering way through Hadnall. We chose the quieter way which led through quaint hamlets and over the gently lifted Hawkstone Hills to send us swinging along to fair Salop, the narrow lanes choked with holiday traffic. One could linger a long time here, amongst the beautiful old houses and churches, the alleys, the

Fig. 70: Lord Hill's Column, Shrewsbury

MUCH WENLOCK.

Fig. 71: Much Wenlock

pulsing life of the present as well as the past, but we pushed on with an
avowal – since redeemed – of further attentions. The road we chose led past
the tall monument to Lord Hill, about whom we can find nothing to justify
such an elevated pedestal, one much higher that he probably had during his
life. We followed, broadly, the upper valley of the Severn which takes a
great sweep on its way to Bridgenorth. There was much to tempt us off our
chosen road, such as the signpost to Homer. We had tea in a typical Mid-

land village, warm, half-timbered houses, gardens already ablaze with flowers – Cressage. In the early evening we dipped to Harley and commenced the long climb up Wenlock Edge. The country northward fell away into a sweeping vista of rich lands, woods, farms and villages, the strongly beating yeoman lands of Severn, oft-contended, saturated with history, and worthy of it all. Just over the summit we stepped into medieval England, the lovely little town of Much Wenlock.

Already dusk was falling; reluctantly, with no more than a slow amble through the streets, past the entrance to the Abbey, we pushed on, along the quiet Bridgenorth road, and in the chilly twilight turned down a lane to Acton Round, where we quickly obtained a campsite. A damp morning. In our snug hollow we repaired a recalcitrant three-speed, lingered half a morning away with leisurely packing, and, becaped, a high wind driving across, continued our journey. At Morville the rain cleared. Slung high in the orchard trees of an old farmhouse, and swinging in the wind, we saw many, many mistletoe boughs and Jo also found white primroses growing wild there. After lunch we joined a lane route just avoiding Bridgenorth, which led us on swinging roads through the copse and thin birches of Wyre Forest. A westwards turn took us to Cleobury Mortimer, with away westward, the high, quarried Clee Hills. A modern town with two lovely black and white inns, and nothing more to hold us. Then we took a crazy way by hilly lanes just because the signposted names attracted us. And Jo's mind was set on Mamble when she discovered it was not far away. At tea in a little cottage at the lovely down-along hamlet of Neen Sollars we studied the map, and found it, only two or three miles away. Jo recited:

"I never went to Mamble
That lies above the Teme,
So I wonder who's in Mamble
And whether people seem
Who brood and breed along there
As lazy as the name…… "

So we went to Mamble, perched far up on a hill. Just an ordinary small village, it was, and I remarked to Jo that she would have done better not to go and retain the illusion, as the poet, Drinkwater had. Now it was:

"……a Mamble broken
That was lissom in a dream."

Our travelling is full of such lissom dreams shattered, and yet how many remain! There is our recently-acquired Homer, and Wig-Wag, and Annalong, and that most romantic-sounding place, Ruyton of the Eleven Towns. That, at least, after many years of careful avoidance, yet eager approach, lies a *"Mamble broken"*! Jo concluded the argument by concluding the poem:

"Who travels Worcester county
Takes any place that comes
When April tosses bounty
To the cherries and the plums."

We hadn't realised it, yet we were in Worcester County. "So it's the cherries and the plum blossoms, because we're in April", said Fred, and away we went in search of blossom. Up again to Clows Top, then a sweep down past a huge, spacious estate, to the aristocratic-sounding name of Shelsley Beauchamp, and the famous river Teme. In this lovely valley we saw no blossom, but we found, at the quiet hamlet of Shelsley Walsh, the most beautiful old house. It was hidden from the road, and we were lucky to find it, along an old lane, until we looked down upon a timber-framed manor house with a green lawn and sheltering yews of great age, all like a dream of Tudor fairyland. We went inside the small church, but gathering dusk made the interior indeterminate.

Fred punctured, and we, like children, sat on a wall eating cream-filled Easter eggs until he came, then we rode hard down the valley in search of a campsite. A huge farm called Ham Castle gave us a site under the shadow of the tall hop-poles – the Teme valley is famous for hop-growing, and even straw was forthcoming to feather our beds.

Scudding clouds, but a fine morning. With no worries about the miles we were piling up for a return journey, we headed for Worcester, watching all the while for the promised blossom, but we were only at the beginning of April, and there wasn't a sign. In the interval between morning service and afternoon service we explored the grand old Cathedral.

Worcester has had a bishopric since the year 679, and about 980 Oswald built a cathedral on this site. This however was replaced by the beginning of the present building in 1084, by Wulfstan, who was, by the way, the only Saxon prelate allowed to keep his see under William the Conqueror. One cannot help but think that he had suitably accommodated himself to the Norman yoke. It appears that he had his qualms about demolishing Oswald's church, and said:

"Wretches that we are, we presumptuously destroy what the saints have wrought. We neglect souls and labour only to pile up stones".

I would emphasise the last sentence! Now, of Wulfstan's building, only the crypt remains: the rest was destroyed by fire. In 1204 the Cathedral we now see was begun. Again calamity overtook the building, the tower collapsed, and the magnificent Early English tower which soars so grandly above the city was completed about 1370. For upwards of six hundred years this lovely pile has dominated the city. There is a modern appearance to the exterior, owing to the original sandstone weathering badly. The new facing, however, was so carefully done that the result is perfect. Like other Eng-

Fig. 72: Worcester Cathedral

lish cathedrals, all the different periods can be seen in the building. The nave is late Decorated, the two west bays are transitional Norman, the presbytery and Lady Chapel are examples of Early English, and the tower, of course, shows each influence, but dominant is the slender tracery of Early English, which seems to reach far above the 200 feet of stonework. Amongst a wealth of modern carved woodwork are some old misericords. We saw also some fine wall-arcading. There are, of course, very many monuments, one particularly noticeable being of King John in the centre of the Presbytery, all done in gilt. In truth, the Office of Works portrayed a sense of finesse, gilding such a black character! He lies in good company, being buried before the High Altar, between Oswald and Wulfstan. A gruesome touch is added too; in the Northeast transept, under a glass case is a portion of a door with particles of human skin attached, said to have been *"torn from the body of some wretch who was flayed alive for sacrilege".* We

Fig. 73: The Gatehouse, Stokesay Castle

also walked the vaulted cloisters and entering the Chapter House, saw – in the entrance hall – a vaulted ceiling supported by a single column. At the foot of some steps a flat gravestone with the one word "miserimus" inscribed puzzled us. Afterwards we heard that the grave is that of a dean who refused to take an oath of conformity, and was expelled. The grave was placed there "that every one might stamp the harder upon it". The mere two hours were too brief, and when swelling organ-notes warned us of the passage of winged time we reluctantly rode away, crossed the river Severn, and along the Hereford road soon left the 'Faithful City' behind us.

We had a much belated lunch at the crossing of the Teme, at Knightwick Bridge, in a cottage with a lovely show of spring flowers in the window. Away to the southwest reared the abrupt Malvern Hills; we itched to be off exploring them, but there was now no more time to go a-Mamble hunting. We struck hard, hilly country then, to Bromyard, Georgian houses and old inns, and hills beyond, swerving away from Hereford towards Leominster. Over the commons into Herefordshire we went, the fat shire rolling in its richness below and before us. The weather became cold and cloudy; we hurried through Leominster, a lovely Georgian town, and refused to even look at the ballflower-decorated church. Then we saw a signpost pointed to Eardisland, and succumbed once again to the lure of the lanes. With one short evening and one day left we went exploring Herefordshire lanes, in contented bliss. The morrow would take care of itself! A snowstorm came on as we entered Eardisland, a lovely, 'black and cream' village by the smooth Arrow stream. In all the midland shires, surely none offer such perfect examples of timber-framed villages as Herefordshire. The next village was Pembridge, every house a Tudor gem, and a village to linger in… We lingered. Violent storms struck us, and night came on as we wandered on. Again, what's in a name, that sent us to Mortimer's Cross, nothing there now except memories of an old battlefield of the fierce War of the Roses, when English fought English, and turned a verdant countryside into a blood-bath. At Bircher, the next village, we were given a campsite in an orchard, and the good farmer, proud of his ancient house, offered to show us round. We went to sleep with the drumming of the rain and the whip of hail upon the thin fabric of the tents.

The night had been bitterly cold, and we were up betimes, with a hundred and twenty miles of windy roads ahead of us. We had to extricate ourselves from the lanes too, and be determined to turn a blind eye to the allure of signposts. On our way to faster roads came a place with more reminders of the Lancastrian-Yorkist wars, Richard's Castle, now just another teasing name. The rain and wind contested our crossing of the Shropshire border. Still 'on tour' we could not hurry through Ludlow, one of the most pleasing of our English Medieval towns, so pregnant with the history of its great castle, its beautiful church, its many quaint inns, including one, probably the most picturesque in England, the 'Feathers'. Another self-promise, since redeemed, was of a long stay in Ludlow.

Then we found ourselves at Stokesay Castle, nor could we resist a look around the strangest fortified manor house in Britain, a lovely specimen of

Fig. 74: The Banqueting Hall, Stokesay Castle

its type. In this is the perfect link between the medieval castle and the period when Britain, becoming more peaceful, began to build homes as homes and not as places of refuge and warlike bases. We read that in 1291 Lawrence de Ludlow obtained a Royal licence to strengthen and crenellate his mansion of stone and lime – the real castle of Stokesay. Little seems to have been recorded of the history of this, which must have seen something of the stormy centuries of border warfare which followed. Then the country became united under the stable government of the House of Tudor. In this flour- ishing period of 'Merrie England' arose those lovely old halls and the gracious houses and villages which are our heritage today. In the days of

The Elizabethan addition to the North Tower. STOKESAY CASTLE.

Fig. 75: North Tower, Stokesay Castle

Elizabeth the highly picturesque timbered addition to the North Tower was built, and the beautiful gatehouse sketched above. Even this has its im- mensely strong door loopholed for musketry. As a manor house Stokesay escaped the fate meted by Cromwell to so many castles, and we have inside a good example of how our forebears lived in Tudor times, from the stone severity of the North Tower to the simplicity of the Great Hall, and the pan- elled and carved richness of the Solar Room.

We rode hard from Stokesay, through drenching showers and against a high wind. Little Stretton, Church Stretton, then Shrewsbury again, for lunch in an ancient, rambling, raftered house. Our return to Whitchurch was by Wem, the main road north, through rich Shropshire farming country, and on quiet roads too, considering the fact that this was Easter Monday.

For our last Cheshire miles – the hurried return following the outward route – the wind cleared the sky, and the sun shone warmly, brightening the thin green shimmer of the new season over the land.

Journey into Medieval England.

"Where England of the
motley states
Deepens like a garden to the
gates
In the purple hills of Wales."

After Bosworth

Fig. 76: After Bosworth

The heart of Medieval England in the first noon of a holiday. Bustling pavements beneath overhanging gables; the confusion of a crowded market place with its stalls, barrows, and the countryfolks with large baskets; narrow streets and twisting alleys carrying the strange names of a proud and ancient past; quiet, reflective backwaters where antique churches stand, their slender spires reaching heavenward, still looking down on the world of men; a grim castle still lording hoary walls over the town; a noble river below, spanned by two bridges of many arches.

Beyond, a countryside equally rich in tradition and event, the very foundations of a great, virile nation. Scenes of military prowess—a feudal England, a land of bright accoutrements and dark deeds. Rich agricultural land, a yeoman, honest, hardworking England. Yeoman of the soil, yeomen of the staple.

During one short week we are to seek out such an England, which, in part at least, still exists amongst the complexities of modern civilisation.

And if aught else great bards
beside
In sage and solemn tones have
sung
Of tourneys, and of trophies
hung,
Of forests, and enchantments
drear,
Where more is meant than
meets the ear.
Milton.

Trial by Ordeal
Under Saxon and
Norman Rule.

Fig. 77: Trial by Ordeal Under Saxon and Norman Rule

There is great fascination about an old English market town, particularly on market days or Saturday afternoon. Bustling streets beneath overhanging gables; the confusion of a crowded market place with its stalls, barrows, and the country folks with their large baskets of produce, cool butter, large clean eggs, delicious cheese and fresh greens; narrow streets and twisting alleys carrying the strange names of a proud and ancient past – all these, as I have outlined overleaf thrilled our eyes as we joined the throng, and jostled our way to a market café for lunch. We were all eyes and ears; we soaked ourselves in the glamorous atmosphere, still intense with pulsing life.

For how many centuries had the feet of wayfarers plodded up and down the jumbled town on every conceivable errand, not always honest! For there was a town here when the ancient Britons prowled the land; they real-ised its natural strength, and fortified the narrow neck of land where the en-girdling river almost meets. To them this was a Pengwern, the 'Hill of Alders'.

Possessed in time by the dark Celts, it became 'Amwythig', until they, in turn, were driven away by the Romans, who made a stronger link of it. The pageant of history marches gallantly forward; now the harsh Saxon gar-risoned and settled the town; their name, 'Scrobbes-byrig', the City in the Shrubs, survives to this day. The proud Norman conqueror built the castle, the succeeding English Marcher lords enlarged it, and Shrewsbury knew no security through the bloody medieval centuries of Plantagenet, Tudor, and Stuart, until the Restoration.

And all through a thousand years the fierce Celt hovered in the background of his native hills, pouncing, slaying, burning, looting – and withdrawing to his inaccessible mountains. For two thousand years and more, watchful sentinels of many races paced their ramparts even as we paced – but with far more zeal and keener perception, towards the lovely, danger-pregnant hills of Wales.

Today, however, one sees the sheer beauty of peaceful art, lovely old houses built in an age of growing commerce, monastic glories, and the cultural associations of a famous school. Gems of Tudor house building are everywhere; in the most unexpected places, down alleys, hidden behind Victorian buildings less worthy, illuminating the happier period that lies between the long Border wars and modern times. In an expectant spirit one happily searches out odd corners and with delight discovers strange street names; Wyle Cop, Frankwell, Dogpole, Mardol, Pride Hill, Butcher Row, Grape Lane. What stories the very names can tell! Sometimes a fragment is borne on metal plates, as those which tell their tale at the Castle Street – High Street junction. They read as follows:

"Near this place, at the junction of these three streets was the High Cross, taken down in 1687. There the Earl of Worcester, Sir Robert Venables, and Sir Richard Vernon, were executed on Monday 23 July 1403, after the Battle of Shrewsbury fought on the 21st, and the dead body of Henry Percy 'Hotspur' was here placed between two millstones and afterwards beheaded and quartered.

June, 1941.

" High the vanes of Shrewsbury gleam
Islanded by Severn stream;
The bridges, from the steepled crest
Cross the water, east and west."

Gateway House

Fig. 78: Gateway House, Shrewsbury

Near this spot David III, Prince of Wales, was executed 3rd October 1283. He was tried for high treason by Parliament which met at Shrewsbury, September 30th 1283. He was sentenced to be hung, drawn and quartered. This was the first Parliament in which the Commons were represented. London and 20 other cities (including Shrewsbury) each returned two Burghers."

(Grope Lane.

Fig. 79: Grape Lane, Shrewsbury

In the Battle of Shrewsbury here mentioned, Hotspur was killed on the field, and a sideline of the times, when even dead bodies came in for revengeful and useless mutilation, helps one to understand the passions roused by internecine strife. This battle consolidated Henry IV, the first Lancastrian, on the throne, paving the way to the disastrous Wars of the Roses, and profoundly changing the whole course of English History.

Many houses are sunk deep in history as well as streets. There is that lovely example of 16th century half timbered architecture, the Council House, one time Court of the Lord Marchers, a lodging place of Henry VIII, and of Charles I. There is a house on the descent of Wyle Cop where Henry VII stayed in 1485 just prior to his final and brilliant victory over Richard III at Bosworth Field. There is Rowley's House too, an isolated gem of timber work.

For even greater beauty and more venerable age, St Mary's Church in a quiet backwater, dates back to Norman times. Perhaps the finest feature there is the wealth of richly stained glass, and best of all a Jesse window, six hundred years old, sheds its soft radiance down the nave. There are many quaint and interesting memorials, some of which we copied, and are set down here. This over the main door, on the outside:

"Let this small monument record the name
Of Cadman, and to future times proclaim

How by'n attempt to fly from this high spire
Across the Sabrine stream he did acquire
His fatal end. Twas not for want of skill
Or courage to perform the task he fell.
No, no, a faulty cord being drawn too tight
Hurried his soul on high to take her flight
Which bade the body here beneath, good night.

Feb 2, 1739 Age 28"

Truly a pioneer of aerial flight!

Puzzle this out, I'm afraid we failed! Inside the porch, a brass tablet:

"Here Lyeth the body of Mrs Sarah Phillips
Interred by her first husband, John Price, Gent,
She had to her second husband, Thomas
Phillips, Gent, and dyed his widow.

25 January 1733. Aged 54"

Fig. 80: Fish Street, Shrewsbury

There are tablets also to Admiral Benbow and Samuel Butler, who were both natives of Shrewsbury. In modern times worthy men have also been bred in the town. The statue of Charles Darwin stares over the same streets where, as a boy, he gave no clue to a future which was to startle the world with a proven theory of cosmic change. Here is the Silver of Mary Webb, who sold her garden produce from a stall, and jostled with the Saturday throngs. A. E. Houseman, 'The Shropshire Lad', sang his sad songs of the old town, and, in inspired verse, brings back to life those wild, far-off days of the Celtic twilight:

"The flag of morn in Conqueror's state
Enters at the English gate;
The vanquished ever, as night prevails
Bleeds upon the road to Wales"

Fig. 81: The Marches from Offa's Dyke

NB: p. = multiple page entries   pp. = consecutive page entries

JPMPF Publication List

- *Lightweight Cycle Catalogue Volume 1*; (2005)
- *An Encyclopaedia of Cycle Manufacturers* - by Ray Miller; (2006)
- *Frederick H Pratt and Sons* - Complete Cycle Engineers - Alvin J E Smith; (2006)
- *The Electric-Powered Bicycle Lamp 1888-1948* - Peter W Card; (2006)
- *The Pedersen Hub Gear* - Cyril J Hancock; (2007)
- *It wasn't that Easy. The Tommy Godwin Story* - Tommy Godwin; (2007)
- *The End to End & 1000 Miles Records* - Willie Welsh; (2007)
- *Lightweight Cycle Catalogue Vol II;* (2007)
- *Origins of Bicycle Racing in England* - Andrew Ritchie; (2007)
- *Here Are Wings* - Maurice Leblanc (Translation by Scotford Lawrence); (2008)
- *The Origins of the Bicycle* - Andrew Ritchie; (2009)
- *Lightweight Cycle Catalogue Vol III*; (2009)
- *East Anglian Rides* - Charles Staniland, Edited by Gerry Moore; (2009)
- *The Stanley Show, Review* 1878 to 1889 & Catalogue 1890; (2009)
- *Flying Yankee* - The International Career of Arthur Augustus Zimmerman - Andrew Ritchie; (2009)
- *An Encyclopaedia of Cycle Manufacturers* - 2nd Edition- by Ray Miller; (2009)
- *Cycle History 19*- Proceedings of the 19th ICHC, Saint-Etienne, France, 2008; (2010)
- *Cycle History 20* - Proceedings of the 20th ICHC, Freehold, New Jersey, USA 2009; (2010)
- *Boneshaker Reprints Vol 5, Issues 41-50;* (2010)
- *The Veteran-Cycle Club 1955-2005* - by Cyril Hancock; (2010)
- *A History of the Tricycle* - Roger Alma, Cyril J Hancock and Derek Roberts; (2011)
- *Marque Album No. 1 Centaur* - Alvin Smith & Lionel Ferris; (2011)
- *Cycling History No. 1, Malvern Cycling Club 1883-1912* - Roger Alma; (2011)
- *Marque Album No. 2, Ivel* - Ray Miller & Lee Irvine; (2011)
- *Dan Albone, Cyclist, Inventor & Manufacturer.* - Ray Miller & Lee Irvine; (2011)
- *Cycling History No. 2 - Vol. 1, Rough Stuff, The Charlie Chadwick Story* - David Warner; (2012)
- *Cycling History No. 2 - Vol. 2, Further Adventures, The Charlie Chadwick*

Story - David Warner; (2013)

- *Marque Album No. 3, Rensch-PARIS* - Alvin Smith et al; (2012)
- *Cycling History No. 3 - Vernon Blake 1875-1930* - Steve Griffith; (2012)
- *Cycling History No. 4 - Charlie Davey* - Christine Watts; (2012)
- *Lightweight Cycle Components, Volume 1* - Steve Griffith; (2013)
- *Cycling History No. 5 - Herne Hill* - John Watts; (2013)

All publications are available through the Veteran-Cycle Club Sales Officer. www.v-cc.org.uk

This second Charlie Chadwick volume takes us much further into his adult life and indeed starts with his best story 'Two – A Tandem and a Tyre'. This relates how in 1929 Charlie persuaded his friend Joe (who owned a tandem) to leave his girlfriend behind and become Charlie's 'stoker' for ten days in the southwest of England. It speaks volumes for Charlie's power of persuasion! Their subsequent adventures read like that old classic comedy book 'Three Men in a Boat'.
www.charliechadwick.org

The Veteran-Cycle Club
Cycling History Series No 2
© 2014 JPMPF
ISBN 978-0-9575628-1-3

ROUGH · STUFF · FELLOWSHIP

· JOHN PINKERTON · MEMORIAL PUBLISHING FUND ·

VETERAN-CC